"Stepping On My Brother's [Head] Other Secrets Your English Professor Never Told You

A College Reader

Edited by
Sondra Perl and Charles Schuster

Boynton/Cook Publishers
HEINEMANN
Portsmouth, NH

Boynton/Cook Publishers, Inc.
361 Hanover Street
Portsmouth, NH 03801–3912
www.boyntoncook.com

Offices and agents throughout the world

The authors and publisher wish to thank those who have generously given permission to reprint borrowed material: "Just Like in Benheim" by Mimi Schwartz Copyright ©2009 by Mimi Schwartz. Reprinted by permission of the author.

Library of Congress Cataloging-in-Publication Data
Stepping on my brother's head and other secrets your English professor never told you : a college reader / edited by Sondra Perl and Charles Schuster.
     p. cm.
    Includes bibliographical references.
    ISBN-13: 978-0-86709-592-0
    ISBN-10: 0-86709-592-X
    1. College readers.   2. Literature—Collections. I. Perl, Sondra.
II. Schuster, Charles.
    PE1417.S753 2010
    808'.0427—dc22   2009046896

Editor: Lisa Luedeke
Production editor: Sonja S. Chapman
Cover design: Night & Day Design
Compositor: Aptara®, Inc.
Manufacturing: Valerie Cooper

Printed in the United States of America on acid-free paper
14   13   12   11   10   VP   1   2   3   4   5

Contents

Bloom describes the sisterhood of women who share locker room conversations about family, life, health. The essay ends with Bloom recounting a near-rape experience that occurred in a Swedish locker room, one which traumatized her but also reinforced her view about the importance of community.

Spinner begins by confessing that she is "a college drop-out. Or I was. Now I am an English professor." Her poignant essay reveals the shame she felt when she dropped out of college and the struggle she went through to gain independence, both of which now enable her to respect and understand the fears, tribulations, and triumphs experienced by many of her own students.

Ballenger confesses that now, as a 50-something adult, he realizes he is "not as dumb as I thought." Ballenger refreshingly rehearses the childhood incidents and events that persuaded him he was not smart, or not smart enough, discusses intellectual bullies, and explains his slow transition if not to "smartness" then at least to "smart enough."

Malinowitz describes the relationship between writing and the self, how we author our selves out of the very texts we write about ourselves, but her primary focus is on a book she read as a young woman and how, later in her life, she rediscovers the author, writes to her, and ends up in a serious and loving relationship with her—all through email, writing, and language.

With an emphasis on the trials and joys of motherhood, Eldred tells of her two adopted Russian sons, one of whom fills his life with lies that both hide and reveal the truths and feelings he carries—and how a loving and understanding mother responds to the lies, to her two children, and to the question of adoption and the accepted wisdom surrounding the passing on of heritage.

Schwartz's essay captures the immigrant experience, focusing especially on Sophie Marx, who emigrated to America from Benheim, Germany but never altogether left her German town behind. The essay captures Sophie's sense of dislocation mixed with equal doses of comfort and optimism and helps Schwartz catch glimpses of the alluring past of her father who, like Sophie, was also a Benheimer.

Rose narrates important events from his childhood in Altoona, Pennsylvania. Journeying with him, the reader hears the stories that haunt Rose and comes to understand that it is the stories, the secrets, and the revelations from our pasts that shape who we are today.

This is the tragic and mysterious story of Faery's dark-eyed beautiful great-grandmother, Ella Seagroves: "I think in 1906, when Ella would have been maybe twenty-one or so—while Will was at work at the cotton mill one day, she cleaned the house to its usual spotlessness and she bathed little Lonnie, three at the time, and dressed him in clean clothes and took him to a neighbor's. When Will came home she was gone, without a word, and without a trace." Faery does her best to recover this tragic history—and tries to explain why it still resonates with her today.

Through her poems and lyrical confessions, Perl reveals family secrets as she writes about refusing to undergo plastic surgery for a nose job, what it might have meant that her fierce mother-in-law kept a .22 revolver in her bedroom closet, and her own shock when her husband suddenly adopted the trappings of orthodox Judaism. Perl's contribution bends our expectations of genre, combining as it does confession, narrative, and the poetic.

Introduction

Sondra Perl and
Charles Schuster

We have put this book together because we believe that writing is meant to be read with pleasure, with a sense that you, a college student in a writing classroom, are walking down a path looking forward to what you will find around the next bend. Every piece of writing, at its best, should encourage you to peer around that corner while also communicating the passion of the author toward a subject and toward the act of writing itself. Every paragraph and every page should in their focus and phrasing cause you to feel a sense of wonder, to be moved, to be informed, to be transformed, and ideally to want both to continue reading and to start writing. This book was conceived to fulfill those basic, fundamental goals.

All of us in this book teach college writing, often in courses that emphasize (importantly) academic argument, scholarly research, and factual analysis. These modes and strategies underlie work in the academy, but so does the exploration of the self found in narrative prose, autobiography, memoir, and creative nonfiction—what we might want to call "life writing." The essays in this book are intended to offer a range of models for personal exploration, but just as importantly they offer you models and possibilities for your own essays, your own stylistic, rhetorical, compositional development.

The title of this book is *"Stepping On My Brother's Head" and Other Secrets Your English Professor Never Told You* because, in fact, every contributor has revealed a secret. We invited well-known and accomplished college writing teachers to write confessional essays that were revelatory, that took risks both in terms of what they said and how they said it. To us, the word *secret* does not connote shame but rather something hitherto private, untold, or personally prized. We encouraged the authors in this book to explore a secret they recently discovered about themselves, or to describe a secret passion they had kept private but were now willing to share. We asked them to explore where this longing originated, what it meant, and why they have or have not explored it. We wanted the selections to reveal something new, something most students had not heard before or thought of—a life lesson, a moment of surprising insight, a sudden turn from childhood toward adulthood, speculation about what their life would have been like if. . . .

We invite you to read these essays with an eye to the craft used by each writer. We hope you will examine the styles, tones, research perspectives, structures, and rhetorical strategies each writer uses to develop his or her work. We also hope that you will be excited by what you read here, so much so that you will want to write your own "revelation," that you will decide to take a risk, revealing what it is that you have, until now, kept secret—maybe even kept secret from yourself.

Finally, we hope you enjoy reading the essays in this book. Students often ask us how they can learn to be better writers, how they can improve their comfort and confidence as writers, how they can gain fluency and find their own style. There is no easy answer, but the one constant is that good writers read for pleasure. They read stories, great literature, biographies, and intellectually challenging books and articles. They read graphic novels, newspapers, fashion and fishing how-tos, comics, and cookbooks. They read while standing in line at the grocery store and before they fall asleep at night. They read while grabbing a quick bowl of cereal in the morning and while waiting for the bus at the commuter parking lot. Because writers read for pleasure, they take advantage of every opportunity to read a few more pages or one more chapter before the bus arrives or the class starts. In doing so, they gain an increasingly rich and intuitive understanding of how different writers compose. They internalize the rhythms of polished and public language. They become readers who slowly but steadily learn how writing moves them, how stories, essays, and poems are crafted by accomplished writers. Ultimately, they absorb a multitude of styles, words, rhythms, and rhetorical strategies, and in doing so they learn what will work for them in their own composing. Every good writer reads (and reads a lot) for pleasure.

We hope you find pleasure and genuine satisfaction in this book. It is why we conceived it, why we and all the contributors wrote our essays, and what we hope stays with you as you take risks, embrace challenges, and discover the satisfactions of the writing life.

As long as we are in a confessional mode, we want to thank Lisa Luedeke who championed this book and kept urging us to do it, Maura Sullivan who gave us our title and contributed limitless market savvy, and Sonja Chapman who navigated the turbulent waters of production while this book went through successive revisions and transformations. Thanks to you all; it has been a pleasure—really!

Sondra Perl, *Lehman College, City University of New York*
Charles Schuster, *University of Wisconsin–Milwaukee*

Stepping On My Brother's Head

Charles Schuster

Charles Schuster is Professor of English and Director of the Honors College at the University of Wisconsin–Milwaukee. A former director of composition and associate dean of the humanities, Professor Schuster has both taken and taught first-year composition as well as more advanced courses in writing and literature. His brother, by the way, has shown no ill effects either as a result of the events recorded in this essay or from reading about them.

Over fifty years ago, I stepped on my brother's head. By confessing now to this painful and unfortunate act, I realize that I am a bit tardy. Time may heal all wounds, but even with the lapse of so many years, it impossible to overstate the severity or psychological significance of a brother stepping on another brother's head. Quite the contrary, stepping on someone's head, whether that head belongs to your brother, another family member, or even just a friend or stranger, is no mean event. It does not go unnoticed, and it cries out for explanation. To say "I'm sorry" doesn't mitigate it; to avoid talking about it, as I have done for years, allows the head trodding event to fester. Among the secrets I have never told anyone—neither my wife, my son, nor my rabbi—this dark moment from my past ranks high, perhaps because its possible meanings potentially echo and reverberate down the long, narrow hallways of my life. Thus it seems time, past time really, to shine a bright light on an act that can probably only be characterized as callous and savage, or, perhaps more to the point, dumb and dumber.

I was nine years old, and my brother, Marty, eleven going on twelve. It was 1954. Dwight D. Eisenhower was president, and America was in the midst of a Cold War with the Soviet Union and a postwar economic boom on the domestic front. The life of my family and me was circumscribed by bomb shelters, dog tags, patriotism, social conformity, segregation, neighborhood schools, and only a scant awareness—at least on my part—of what was happening in the next state, let alone in other countries. News did not enter our lives through the Internet, which lay thirty years into the future, or the television, which was a strikingly new medium. Rather, we learned about events by listening to the radio or reading the Cleveland newspapers, one issued early in the morning and the other slapped on our doorstep or inserted into our milk chute in late afternoon. The world felt slow and safe to me, and I had no idea how it all might shift once I stepped on my brother's head.

I was sitting on the family couch in our modest living room in our modest small home in a working-class neighborhood on the west side of Cleveland, Ohio. My mother and father sat nearby. We were watching television on a small black-and-white Emerson that my parents had bought so that we could enjoy those early delights: *Playhouse 90*, *Sid Caesar's Your Show of Shows*, *Liberace*, *The Howdy Doody Show*, *The U.S. Steel Hour*, *The Ernie Kovacs Show*, *Dragnet*, *The Ed Sullivan Show*. It was the golden age of television, although we didn't know it then. Since the advent of that small black-and-white flickering screen, the living room even more than the kitchen had become the center of our domestic universe. We tried not to let it overwhelm our lives, however, although it did occupy many evenings. I do not mean to suggest that the fascination of watching television, eyes glazed forward, explains or justifies what happened. Not at all. In trodding on my brother's cranial extremity, I wasn't attempting to be Stanley Laurel unknowingly humiliating Oliver Hardy, nor an infuriated Moe acting out revenge on Curly or Larry. In fact, my brother and I were mostly compatible, if quite different in our interests and personalities.

By most standards, certainly today's, we were a fortunate and happy nuclear family. Although we had little money and were only living in this home by the grace of our grandfather's holding the mortgage, my father earned enough money to put food on the table (although on Sunday nights, we were reduced to a dinner of bread and honey, which, not knowing any better, I thought was a treat). We owned a car, an old but reliable Buick, and on weekends we chugged across town to visit a small but devoted circle of aunts, uncles, and cousins. Dad worked six, even seven days a week in my grandfather's cramped, neighborhood hardware store where he would typically spend two hours helping someone plan out their new bathroom drains, cinching the prolonged afternoon discussion by selling thirty cents' worth of pipe joint cement. No wonder the store went out of business ten years later. My father, it's clear, did not care much for material possessions, but he dearly loved his family. On a rare free Saturday or Sunday, he would take mom, my brother, and me to the Rocky River Reservation for a family picnic where after dinner we would hunt for tadpoles or wander through the woods in search of garter snakes. Unlike many of my friends' fathers, Dad did not hang out with his high school buddies in a bar or play poker in some neighbor's garage. He spent his free time with us. He and my mother would save and scrimp for years so that they could take us on car trips, one each to Niagara Falls, Miami Beach, and Yellowstone National Park. Whether we were driving across town or across the country, my brother and I would sit in the cavernous backseat of the car in relative harmony, identifying exotic license plates (from Kentucky, Iowa, or Georgia), playing word games, counting cows, and either shivering in the winter or sweating in the summer. Occasionally we would punch each other or start squabbling; our dad would warn us and then, hanging onto the steering wheel with his left hand, randomly swat at us with his long right arm until we reverted to our usual docile state. On the longer trips, my brother would occasionally get promoted by my father to the front seat in order to navigate, an important responsibility he earned because of his elder status and his seriousness of purpose, the front seat being no place for a frivolous younger brother. Exchanging places with my mother, Marty would climb up front, unfold the map, and start plotting out a direct route from Bay Village to Toledo or from Omaha, Nebraska to Rapid City, South Dakota. In those days, there were no turnpikes, no freeways, just little squiggly lines wandering across folded map pages and through America's countryside, lines that needed careful tracing with a thoughtful and scrupulous forefinger.

With my father away so much working and managing the neighborhood hardware store, mom remained at home, taking care of Marty and me, cooking, cleaning, and managing the household affairs. She loved us, but she found raising two boys challenging and frequently infuriating. Her exasperation led to sustained verbal outbursts, which I described to Marty as "the devil's bellows." On the worst days, when Marty and I created some terrible mayhem such as sassiness or going over to Billy and Denny's house and not telling my mother where we were, my father would come home, hear the latest outrage, and then swat us on the rear end with an old, long, black plastic shoehorn. He said it hurt him more than us, but I couldn't figure out how that could possibly be.

Mom cooked dinner every night: spaghetti with sauce straight out of the can, meatloaf with a mustard-ketchup-brown sugar glaze, roast chicken bathed in barbecue sauce, green beans compressed into green mush by the pressure cooker. And she was an obsessive cleaner. She scrubbed the kitchen floor every week on her hands and knees, vacuumed constantly, and not only washed our clothes after soaking them in bleach but also ironed the entire family's shirts, pants, socks, towels, washcloths, and handkerchiefs. That's how I learned to iron, by practicing on my and my brother's socks. Mom never saw something made out of cotton that she didn't feel needed immediate heating and flattening.

I offer this brief description of mom and dad to explain that I harbored no visceral antagonism toward them—or for that matter toward my brother, about whom I will shortly say more. Life was good. During the school year I attended our neighborhood public school, following in the footsteps of my brother. In the evenings I did homework after eating dinner with my family, often lying on the living room floor working out math problems while listening to AM radio. Weekends we frequently played four-handed pinochle or drove east along the lake front, where (in those days) trash fires burned day and night, casting a red glow against the darkening sky. Ultimately we arrived in Cleveland Heights or Beechwood to visit grandparents, aunts, uncles, and cousins. Summers, my brother and I played street baseball with neighborhood friends or moved inside to try our luck at canasta or a challenging game of Monopoly. In nice weather, I wandered over to the nearby woods with my butterfly net and clean mayonnaise jar to collect insects, occasionally getting a soaker when I stumbled into the creek. Life was good. True, my teachers often compared me unfavorably to my brother: he was the focused and mature one; I was the class clown who wandered aimlessly through some inner space. True, my mother thought my brother intellectually capable, while remaining convinced I was retarded until one of my Sunday school teachers told her I had promise, even if my thinking was a bit scattered. True, my brother drank out of a glass before he could walk while I would have continued to suck on a bottle until I went to college if my mother hadn't thrown away all the nipples in the house. And yes, it is true that my beloved Uncle Leo praised my brother for his industry and foresight while accusing me of being lazy and inconsequential, which I wasn't, at least not all that much. But those are only minor blemishes on an otherwise quiet and harmonious life.

As is clear, Marty was my solid and serious older brother. He was constantly praised for having a good head on his shoulders, a fact I must have ultimately found annoying. A good student with interests in science and math, he was three years ahead of me in school and worked many weeknights and weekends with my father in the hardware store, mastering complex mechanical feats such as wiring overhead light fixtures and cutting and threading pipe. By the age of eleven, he knew more about replacing faucet stems, beveling two-by-fours, cutting glass, and rewiring Philco radios than Mr. Fixit. Working with dad, Marty would reseal the first floor toilet or install an automatic screen door closer faster than I could untie the knots in my tennis shoes. He had genuine affection for me in an older brother sort of way, but he also had his own small circle of friends with whom he played chess, hearts, and occasionally tennis. Being so different from one another, we did not really compete. He spent a lot of time with Dad; I spent a lot with Mom. He worked; I read science fiction novels. He practiced on his school violin dutifully every night, torturing those strings during "Captain Video"; I desultorily played the accordion and then the tuba, proving proficient in neither.

I never felt that he was more favored by my parents, not really. In fact, I was the spoiled younger brother, even though my mother kept reminding me that she almost died delivering me, and that within days of my birth in Mt. Sinai Hospital, I had contracted impetigo and caused her a boatload of anguish. In many ways, I became the "daughter" she never had, and it didn't take me long to demonstrate my status, especially at the dinner table. Since we were poor and Jewish, we ate a lot of foods other families rejected: cheap cuts of brisket, roasted for fourteen hours in a four hundred–degree oven; boiled chicken feet; slow-cooked beef tongue, usually sliced and served on rye bread with mustard; and the ever-abhorrent liver, fried hard in Crisco until it had the consistency of tree bark. My mother never saw a chicken she didn't think needed desiccating in an uncovered roasting pan at four hundred degrees for most of a Sunday. No vegetable escaped her kitchen without being wholly atomized. Whereas my brother was an omnivore and ate everything on his plate, no matter its color and consistency, I was much more discerning. I ate almost no fruits or vegetables, would allow nothing green on my plate, detested ketchup, mayonnaise, and mustard, and subsisted primarily on RC Cola, plain hamburgers, and Hostess cupcakes with the surprise inside. Marty, meanwhile, ate everything but the paper napkins.

Dinner was a frequent battleground. "Eat your spaghetti," my mother would say, pointing to my plate. "But there are little things in the sauce," I'd complain and then commence to pick out every piece of mushroom and onion I could find. Meanwhile, as I chewed on one end of a strand of pasta, my brother and father would heap their plates a second time.

Perhaps my problem, if problem it was, could be described as an overactive imagination. In those days, I lived mostly in my own head, which by the way I had never placed in a position where it might be stomped on by friend or foe. My fantasy life was vivid, in retrospect, perhaps as a counterpoint to my day-to-day life, which was safe and comfortable if dull (I remember long periods of staring out the window). To compensate, I read voraciously—reams of action comics: Blackhawk, Superman, Batman, and Green Arrow; tons of pop fiction: A. E. Van Vogt, Robert Heinlein, Luke Short, Tom Swift. I doted on *Alice in Wonderland* and *Through the Looking Glass*, each of which I read at least seven or eight times (I clearly identified with Alice, which may account for my feminist leanings). Action narratives utterly absorbed me. I enacted elaborate and immature melodramatic plots that unfolded inside my brain while I pretended to look outward into the world. I may have been helping a weekend customer in the hardware store find a #8 flathead galvanized wood screw, but in reality I was facing an evil cowboy (who bore a remarkable resemblance to Jack Palance of *Shane*) in a merciless showdown. On the home front, when my mother asked me to take out the garbage or vacuum the hallway, I did so slowly, without alacrity, not because I hated to work but as a result of my having been transported somehow to another world where I was wrestling with a Gortimede green alien on a cliff edge overlooking the Wasnznat Territorial Compound on Neptune or propelling magnetic force beams from my sonic canon at a marauding space cruiser. Sure I played baseball on our neighborhood side street and football on the large lawn near John Marshall High School, but many of my most engaged moments were spent laying out elaborate scenarios with my miniature soldiers, cowboys, and Indians in the backyard, blowing up dirt encampments with firecrackers my father bought for us during our Florida trip, or waving my plastic sword at Basil Rathbone and his despicable minions in the damp basement of our modest brick bungalow while artlessly dodging the ironing board and mimeograph machine.

None of this explains, however, how I could step on my brother's head, even if that head was lying on the floor at my feet, especially since it was attached to my brother's neck, body, arms, and legs. All of him, that is, was lying on the floor watching the same television show as were my parents and I. I do not remember what that show was, but it must have been on in early evening. Maybe it was *Gunsmoke* or *The Red Skelton Show*. The living room was well lit, so I lack the excuse of darkness and obscurity. Nor did my brother somehow slide himself and his head secretly and surreptitiously from a neighboring chair onto the floor without my notice. Not at all. In the back of my mind I knew he was there, lying on the floor below the couch, occasionally propping his head up on an elbow, sometimes lying down entirely on our carpet—knew it without really being very conscious of the fact, it now seems to me. I was similarly reclining comfortably on the couch, my shoes off, my legs stretched out at one end, my head safely propped up at the other, high off the floor.

Suddenly, I felt the need to get up, perhaps to go into the kitchen for something to drink or to reimmerse myself in a Green Lantern comic book. I remember swinging my legs over the edge of the couch and putting my right foot down. Somehow, inexplicably, the floor felt higher, a good distance higher but that didn't bother me. In my life, rising floors, like ray guns and dematerialization machines, were everyday occurrences. I stepped firmly down, and the floor beneath my stockinged foot felt both higher and rounder, even a bit yielding. But I had decided to get up and get up I did, putting my full weight on my right foot as I swung my left foot forward.

There must have been a scream, a yell, a shout of outrage. There must have been crying, and the soothing hands of parents trying to calm an aggrieved and wounded older son and loving brother. But for me, peering at this event down the long tunnel of time, I remember nothing other than the feel of that head beneath my cotton-covered foot. All I can say in my own defense is that it did not feel like a head, but then again it did not feel like the floor either. I stood stunned in the living room as my parents soothed and comforted Marty, who thankfully did not suffer serious physical damage. How could this have happened? Why didn't I realize that it was a living human head, not a carpeted floor, upon which I stood? And when I was punished (out came that long, black shoehorn), I—dare I say it—felt innocent. I had not intended to step on his head. His head was not supposed to be on the floor; it was supposed to be on his neck, upright, where I could see it. It couldn't be my fault; I was doing what any boy would do who wanted to step off the couch. For God's sake, stepping on your brother's head could happen to anybody!

Actually, when examined in the cold light of adulthood, not really. In poll after anonymous poll, typically conducted during professorial dinners or late-night poetry readings with friends and colleagues, not one of them has stepped on his brother's head. Nor can they conceive of it as a possibility, regardless of whether the head might belong to a brother, sister, cousin, close friend, or total stranger. "You must be joking!" is a typical response. Or the rhetorical question, "How could you—how could anyone—possibly do that? You must have really hated your brother." These responses have given me pause and have compelled me to do what any professor would do, namely to think about the event and marshal my research skills for analysis and insight.

Maybe, for example, I was sick of being the younger son, the finicky eater, the favorite of his mother, the one who often charmed his way out of most of life's sordid scrapes and unforeseen miseries. Maybe I wanted to do something bold that would get me in serious trouble from which extrication was impossible—and had decided that the best way to accomplish this would be to take a giant step for humankind right in front of both my parents. That's it—I just wanted to get myself punished, like any nine-year-old guilt-ridden masochist.

No, that can't be right. I think there must be a simpler solution, one that hearkens back six thousand years as I had recently been learning in fourth-grade Sunday school. We had been reading the Old Testament, working through various Bible stories and talking about the ethical dimensions of the choices different Biblical personae had made, people like Abraham who was willing to sacrifice his own son and Moses punishing the Jews at Mount Sinai for worshipping the golden ram. And then, most problematic of all, was the story of Cain and Abel, that short, frightening narrative of sibling rivalry. Could that be at the root of my savagery? Psychologist Jane Leder explores this subject in *Psychology Today* (Jan/Feb 1993, to be precise). The article may be over fifteen years old, but it still unnerves me, for Leder quotes another psychologist, British researcher Judy Dunn, who concludes that:

> From 18 months on siblings understand how to comfort, hurt, and exacerbate each other's pain. They understand family rules, can differentiate between transgressions of different sorts, and can anticipate the response of adults to their own and to other people's misdeeds.

By age three, children have a sophisticated grasp of how to use social rules for their own ends. They can evaluate themselves in relation to their siblings and possess the developmental skills necessary to adapt to frustrating circumstances and relationships in the family. Whether they have the drive to adapt, to get along with a sibling whose goals and interests may be different from their own, can make the difference between a cooperative or rivalrous relationship.

Cooperative? Rivalrous?? This is the brother who looked after me, who shouldered responsibilities so I could fritter away my time, who ran into the street in front of an oncoming car on Rudyard Road to rescue me from a fight when I was three years old. This is the brother who taught me how to play marbles and sparked my interest in science when he reassembled the skeleton of a large (and thankfully dead) turtle. In stepping off that sofa, was I declaring my intent to tear that relationship asunder? Was I a working-class citizen Cain?

Or maybe I have the wrong Bible narrative in mind, maybe the story that influenced me was Jacob stealing the birthright from his older (I said "older"!!) brother, Esau. After all, I wasn't my father's favorite (at least I wasn't at all sure that he loved me better). I could not turn a gasket or calk a socket. Instead of learning to cut glass, I hid in the hardware store basement. My worst mistake was taking a huge packet of incoming mail that included dozens of our own invoices with payment checks—and mailing it. It thus is not surprising that my dad failed at times to appreciate me. He did not understand when I stuck a shell deep inside my ear better to hear the ocean. He lost patience when I sat on his vintage 78 rpm records. During those cross-country trips, he never asked *me* to navigate! So maybe I had had my fill and decided to express my rage at he who stood between me and my rightful patrimony. If I could rise up, if I could get a-head of Marty, just once, my rightful place in the family would be secure.

Or was it even more Oedipal than that? Was I, a semiconscious young boy, deeply tied to my mother (I was her favorite after all). Did I identify my brother with my father, the man to whom he felt close and to whom he was devoted? My brother toiled in the fields (so to speak) alongside my father while I, the itinerant and foolish younger son, moped around the house reading novels and practicing feints in the furnace room using my rapier in a duel to the death. Oh that short and useless rapier! Unable to strike out at my father, I must have chosen my brother as a convenient and more accessible simulacrum?

Actually, when I think about this incident from another perspective, neither I nor my older brother was at fault. The true guilty parties, the ones who began the chain of events that led to this domestic tragedy, were my parents. At first this theory may seem preposterous, even ludicrous: what possible blame could be assigned to them? The answer lies not in that room but twelve years earlier when they conceived their first child, my brother Marty. From that moment on, the seed was planted, the tangled vine that sprouted in the dark and ultimately bloomed in that living room so long afterward. By being born first and me second, a Darwinian struggle ensued between the two of us. I am relying here, by the way, on the work of the noted scholar, Frank J. Sulloway, recently elected a Fellow of the Association for Psychological Science, in recognition of "sustained outstanding contributions to the advancement of psychological science," according to his current vita. I mention this honor so that his theory is not dismissed as mere conjecture, based as it is on hundreds of historical examples, most notably Charles Darwin (a younger brother, fifth of six siblings; see Sulloway's book, *Born to Rebel*, or his recent article, "Birth Order," in *Family Relationships: An Evolutionary Perspective*, edited by Catherine Salmon and Todd Shackelford, Oxford University Press, 2007, pp. 162–82). Using Darwin as a prime example, Dr. Sulloway believes that personality is deeply tied to birth order, that older siblings identify with authority and are conservative maintainers of order. Younger siblings, by contrast, are radical iconoclasts, wild ones who exceed life's borders. Darwin, like me, was a younger brother! If Sulloway is right, I am blameless. Marty's only problem was being born first; mine, being born second. Stepping onto his head was an expression of my need to defy the stultifying and orderly society that was early 1950s America.

I could explore this incident further, ultimately placing the blame for my podiatric miscue on my obsession with reading novels, some genetic malformation, or my absorption into the romantic idylls of King Arthur or the defeat of Hektor by Achilles before the walls of Troy. Ultimately, however, I want to take responsibility for my own actions;

I want to act like the adult I have inevitably become. So, prompted by the writing of this confessional essay, I called my brother, fifty-three years after the fact. We do not see each other often, but he calls regularly (I less regularly) and checks in on his younger brother. This time, however, I called him, called specifically to apologize. The phone rang a few times, I spoke briefly to his wife, and then he picked up the call, happy to hear from his younger brother. After our initial greeting, I told him I had something I wanted to say, something that has been festering for years. "I just wanted to tell you, Marty," I said, not wanting to lose my nerve, "that I'm sorry for that time long ago when I stepped on your head." There was silence at first as he took this in. I responded quickly, "I hope you will accept my apology, even if it is decades late?" A shorter pause, and then he said, "To be honest, I don't know what you are talking about. As far as I know, you never stepped on my head. It sounds preposterous. How could it ever have happened?"

I do not know how to answer—not then, not now. Did it happen? I can feel my brother's head beneath my foot, I can almost hear his yelp of anguish, I can see the entire event as it unfolds. This visual and sensory evidence, however, is all embedded within my memory, a notoriously unreliable source. My brother, the only witness still alive, remembers nothing and believes that I have made this up, that I am like the governess in "The Turn of the Screw" and am manufacturing my own ghostly Quint. Perhaps the larger question is: does it matter? How do we construct the stories, the characters and events, that narrate our lives? Is the reality of my memory any less influential a factor in my life than the reality of an actual event? What does it mean, whether it happened or not, to step on your brother's head? Perhaps what I most like about this question is that I have yet to resolve it.

Works Cited

Leder, Jane. "Adult Sibling Rivalry," in *Psychology Today*, Jan/Feb 1993; see http://www.psychologytoday.com/articles/199301/adult-sibling-rivalry?page=2.

Sulloway, Frank J. "Birth Order," in *Family Relationships: An Evolutionary Perspective*, edited by Catherine Salmon and Todd Shackelford, Oxford University Press, 2007, pp. 162–82.

Sneaking into
the Movies

Lad Tobin

Lad Tobin teaches English and occasionally directs the First-Year Writing Program at Boston College. When he is not sneaking into movies, he is planning elaborate trips he'll never take, re-sorting his baseball card collection, or going to rock music clubs where he is often the only person without a fake ID. He has written two books of creative nonfiction about teaching creative nonfiction: Writing Relationships *and* Reading Student Writing *(both from Boynton/Cook).*

I've been hiding in the back of theatre 13 in the Regal 15 multiplex for ten minutes and I figure it will be at least twenty minutes more before it's safe for me to come out. I'm here killing time between the end of *The Kite Runner* and the start of *Atonement*, worried that I could arouse the suspicion of the cleaning crew if they were to come in and see me sitting here alone. But this still seems safer than my other options: heading out to the lobby or the concourse where I'd run the risk of running into an usher or ticket taker who may have noticed me earlier in the day or hiding out next door in the party room, a sad-looking, dimly lit, narrow room with a long, narrow table already set with party plates, cups, noise blowers, and hats.

Actually it would probably be safe for me to come out right now since the ushers and ticket takers and cleaners who were here at noon have probably long gone home, but after nine hours of trying hard not to get noticed you lose your bearings.

That's why I'm currently hiding in the dark in theatre 13, but to explain what I've been doing here in the first place, I need to back up.

Think about that scene in all of the caper movies you've ever seen: a group of criminals comes together to talk about how to pull off the perfect crime. There is always a mastermind, some slick guy who lays out the plan, explaining that it will involve staggering risks but even more staggering rewards; there is usually another guy who is an expert at picking locks; there's often a guy who is inhumanly strong and maybe another who is fearless to the point of being a little unstable; and, inevitably, there's some tech-weeny dweeb genius who is an expert with computers or cameras or bugging equipment or explosives.

Then imagine the total opposite: a guy who plans his crime totally on his own. It is a crime with almost no real risk and, even if successful, only about $30 or $40 of reward. And he brings no special skill set to the job. In fact, as a middle-aged, middle-class guy who gets a twinge of nervousness when illegally downloading a song or driving a little over the speed limit, this guy (okay, I admit it, he's me) is particularly ill-suited to be masterminding and executing this crime. In fact, if you heard about someone who got caught sneaking into the movies, I would definitely not be one of the usual suspects.

But for some reason I couldn't stop fantasizing about doing this: I was determined to go to my local fifteen-theatre, multiplex at noon, buy a ticket for the first movie, and then stay to sneak into shows at 2:00, 4:30, 7:00, and 9:45, finally stumbling out into the darkness near midnight, free as a bird.

I'm still not sure I can fully explain why this appealed to me so much: it wasn't as if I was desperately eager to see any or all of the movies on the lists that I spent days compiling and recompiling. And I was much more embarrassed than motivated by the idea of saving the cost of four movie tickets. On the most superficial level, I think I wanted to commit this caper because I knew that I could (which is sort of my own pathetic version of those people who say that they climbed Mt. Everest because it was there) but I think I also wanted to do it because I knew that I shouldn't. Seeing five movies in one day— and sneaking into four of them—is a ridiculous and, for someone of my age, inappropriate thing to do, which, for someone who has gotten tired of trying to do the right and reasonable thing, is part of its appeal. Of course, sneaking into movies is a pretty pathetic way to bust out, as bustouts go: it isn't quitting your job to become a street musician or taking a motorcycle trip down the coast of South America. Still, I have to confess that I get a pleasurable buzz of excitement from deciding to do something that people wouldn't expect of me—or that I wouldn't expect of myself.

In fact, the older I get, the more I chafe at the idea that I should act my age. Which probably explains why once I hit forty I started going to rock music festivals and clubs where I'm the only one in line who doesn't have to show his ID and where the music doesn't even start till after my bedtime. Still, I don't think this movie thing is all about some sort of midlife crisis or fear of mortality: the truth is I've always been drawn to the idea—if not the experience—of excess. When I'm out with family or friends at a Chinese or Indian restaurant, for example, I'm the one in the group who wants to order a dozen different dishes, who worries we won't have enough or that we'll miss out on the best thing on the menu. When our extended family is planning a reunion, I'm the one who worries that a long weekend will be too short for us to feel like we've really connected, and so I'll try to talk everyone into arriving a few days earlier and leaving a few days later. And when I try to figure out why I insist on getting two daily newspapers delivered every single day, I realize that it's not because I actually can or want to read them but because I love waking up to the idea that I could.

The idea of being in a multiplex from noon to midnight, watching big-budget movie after big-budget movie, munching on junk food, relaxing in theatres with cushy, stadium seating, seemed like just the sort of excessive, absurd, age-inappropriate, guilty pleasure I'm increasingly drawn to. But, of course, all of the things that make sneaking into the movies appealing to me—that it is excessive and absurd and age-inappropriate—are also what make me determined not to get caught: if a theatre manager were to catch a fifteen-year-old holding open a side door for a friend or a thirteen-year-old buying a ticket to a PG movie in order to sneak into an R, he or she would probably just call the kid's parents. But if an usher were to notice that I'd been in the theatre all day and were to ask me to show my ticket stub and all I had was one for a noon matinee of, say, *Juno* just as I was walking into, say, the 9:30 showing of *I Am Legend*, I'm not sure what either of us would do or say. I could pretend to be a non-native English speaker who doesn't understand America's customs. "This not okay?" I could say, looking confused. Or I could try to use my age to my advantage by playing the disorientation card: "I must have fallen asleep during the movie. Where am I? What time is it? Are you my mother?"

Knowing I could never pull that off, I decided that the key to this caper was in developing a plan that would keep me in the theatres and out of sight. But coming up with a schedule that would allow me to see five even marginally interesting movies that started and ended at the right times turned out to be way tougher than I expected. Each time I'd put together what seemed like a workable schedule, I'd see that one of the movies on my list ended thirty minutes before or three minutes after the next one. The fact that I was having this much trouble made me wonder and worry whether theatre owners choose movie times specifically to discourage freeloaders from walking out of one movie and walking right into another. But just as my paranoia was starting to take off, I suddenly found a schedule that looked okay: *Cloverfield* at 12:00; *27 Dresses* at 2:00; *Sweeney Todd* at 4:30; *The Kite Runner* at 6:45; and *Atonement* at 9:45.

I knew that this schedule still presented certain challenges: I'd have to find a safe place to hide out during the long gap between *Cloverfield* and *27 Dresses* and then again between *The Kite Runner* and *Atonement.* Like any professional thief or at least any professional thief in a caper movie, I knew that my next necessary step was to "case the joint." So the day before putting my plan into action, I went on a recon mission to the targeted multiplex. With a list of questions in the notebook I had hidden in my coat pocket, I arrived at 2 o'clock for a 2:30 showing of *Juno*, figuring that a half hour would be enough time for me to find out how long the previews and ads lasted before each movie; how quickly the cleaning crew arrived after each movie and how long they spent cleaning the theatre; where the ushers were located; how often they walked through the lobby and theatres; and, most importantly, whether there were any restrooms besides the one in the lobby.

At first I tried to tell myself that this last potential problem wasn't necessarily a make or break thing: if it turned out that there were no other restrooms, I would just cut way down on my beverage consumption (which would also mean cutting way down on my salty food consumption) or I'd summon the nerve to go out to the lobby between movies to use the main restroom and then flash my ticket stub as I hustled back in, pretending I was in the middle of the movie I'd already paid to see. But almost as soon as I had considered those options I knew that they would be unworkable: the very idea that I couldn't use a restroom for twelve hours would make me desperate to get to one within my first twelve minutes. And, given my nervousness in these kinds of situations, I knew that I could pull off the "flash the old ticket stub as if I had just run out to the lobby in the middle of the movie" act once, at most.

Fortunately, my pre-caper recon mission provided me with all of the information I needed. Unfortunately, however, not all of that information was reassuring: I noticed that in addition to the ticket sellers, ticket taker, and concession stand workers, the multiplex had two other employees: a man who looked like he must be the theatre's manager, sitting in a glass booth a half story above floor level, and a young woman who I took to be an assistant manager, scurrying around the lobby, as if on some important, no-nonsense mission. She wore black, formal-looking pants, a white dress shirt, an aqua blue sport coat, and a tiny secret-service-type earplug and mouthpiece. Who, I wondered, could she possibly be listening to and what could they be talking about? A popcorn spill in theatre 6? A counterinsurgency attack on the multiplex by independent theatre owners? A suspicious-looking middle-aged guy with a ticket to *Juno* who was clearly casing the joint for a future crime?

On the bright side, once I got past the ticket taker, I found a small men's restroom tucked between theatres 14 and 15; a water fountain between theatres 1 and 2; and a fancy candy machine next to theatre 8. But just as I started to relax, the blue-coated assistant manager scurried past me, down the concourse, racing past theatres 4, 5, 6, 7, all the while reporting something obviously urgent and important into her mouthpiece. That's when I decided that I would have to dress in layers—maybe not 27 of them but enough so that each time I was in the concourse between theatres, I could sport a slightly different look: from a guy in a green winter coat to a guy in a black hoodie to a fellow in a red flannel shirt to, finally, a man in a baseball cap pulled down so low that it almost covered his eyes.

It's been more than nine hours since I've seen the sky or breathed outside air and, except for one brief but disconcerting Q&A with a cleaning crew guy while I was standing outside theatre 3 ("Did you just see *Cloverfield*? Did you like it?" "Uh, no, not yet; I wasn't just in that theatre. I'm just going now to see a movie"), it's been more than nine hours since I have had a conversation. And it's been almost eight hours since I finished the sandwich I smuggled in but it's only been about twenty minutes since I finally finished the Brobdingnagian-sized popcorn and Diet Coke that I bought when I arrived at noon. More to the point, it's now been almost twenty-five minutes since I came into theatre 13 to kill time before *Atonement*, my fifth and final movie of the day.

Now I know that I'm being paranoid. I can't imagine that anyone who works for this theatre pays much attention to who is going to which movie. But this many hours of hiding can mess with your mind, especially when you're watching movies that churn up all your latent fears and anxieties. I mean, sitting through all the blood and gore and chaos of that monster destroying midtown Manhattan in *Cloverfield* would be enough to creep anyone out even if it weren't for the fact that the whole thing was filmed with a jumpy, handheld camera. Add to that all the blood and gore and weirdness of Johnny Depp cutting people up to make meat pies and then describing it all in Broadway songs in *Sweeney Todd*. *27 Dresses* thankfully provided some lightweight, comic relief though I find I get absurdly tense in all those movies in which a man woos a woman on some false pretense—a bet, a dare, a mix-up, a science experiment—and then ends up falling in love with her. Even though I should know that these movies always work out in the end, I keep worrying about how hurt and angry she'll be when she finds out the truth.

The movie I just saw, *The Kite Runner*, did nothing to settle my nerves, especially those scenes of the main character hiding in the back of a truck as he and his father try to sneak past the guards on the Pakistani-Afghani border. Actually, though, my nerves have been unsettled from the time I arrived this morning at the ticket counter and instead of simply saying "One ticket for *Cloverfield*," I stared up at the giant digital screen displaying all the movie times and titles and, for some reason, pretended that I was trying to decide which movie to see. "Let's see . . . Oh, okay, one for, uh . . . *Cloverfield*. For the, uh, 12 o'clock; yeah, just one ticket." I guess I thought this would make me seem more like someone who had just spontaneously dropped in to see what was playing and less like someone who had spent the previous day casing the joint.

The odd thing is that while my paranoia during the day has gone from bad to worse, my conscience has remained oddly and surprisingly clear. Why aren't I feeling guilty? After all, seeing movies I haven't paid for is clearly wrong. "It's like going into a department store, buying a pair of socks, and stealing a couple of CDs on the way out," my friend said when I asked him if he thought I was doing something wrong. I guess I see his point but for some reason I feel strangely okay with paying for one movie and seeing five. Maybe it's because I'm thinking that after all of the times that I've been overcharged by this multiplex—$9 or $10 for a movie ticket? $6 for a popcorn? $5 for a Coke?—the least they can do is let me see a few movies for free.

In fact, if I wanted to push the idea that the multiplex owes me something, I could point out that I've already sat through hours and hours of advertisements in their theatres for which I was pretty much a captive and unwilling audience. And I'm not even talking about the coming attractions; those I can accept. I'm talking about those commercials that are trying to get me to buy a certain candy, drink a certain soda, wash my hair with a certain shampoo, or hold my company's next corporate meeting in this theatre, before joining the U.S. Marines. It's not hard to see that the multiplexes are double dipping: they are charging us to watch movies while subjecting us to ads that big companies have paid them large sums to run specifically because they know that we'll be in the theatre eager to be excited and entertained.

And I'm not the only person bugged by the whole idea of movie theatres making hundreds of millions of dollars by showing paid ads. Go on the Internet and google "premovie ads" and you'll find dozens of groups organizing complaints, protests, and letter-writing campaigns against this practice. You'll even find that a group of moviegoers once filed a class-action lawsuit against a theatre chain that had taken to running advertisements after the announced starting times of the movies.

Maybe that's why I not only don't feel guilty; I actually feel a certain degree of self-righteousness about my decision, my right, to sneak into the movies. After all, if the multiplexes have decided that it is okay to sell *my* time to advertisers without even asking, then I can decide that it is okay for me to proceed on the assumption that my tickets to these movies have already been paid for—by Audi, Pepsi, Fandango, Target, NBC, the United States Marines, and the National Guard.

And speaking of the National Guard: don't get me started on what I think of that scarily slick, pump up the volume, rock 'n' roll recruiting video that the owners of the multiplex whose theatre I'm now hiding out in have already made me sit through three times today. Intercutting beautifully shot scenes of Revolutionary War–era patriots running through the woods with shots of U.S. soldiers going house to house in what appears to be embattled Baghdad neighborhoods, this video suggests that fighting in a war is not only noble and selfless but also as exhilarating as attending a great rock concert. Would this theatre ever run ads for an antiwar group, I wondered.

But even as I warm up to my own arguments against premovie advertising, I know that I'm rationalizing: after all, I thought of all this justification long after I had made my decision to sneak into these movies. Maybe the real reason I'm not feeling any guilt is that I haven't really enjoyed myself very much. I recognize the illogic of my thinking: whether I've had a good time has nothing to do with whether I've done something wrong or whether I should feel any guilt. But the fact that I now feel almost sick from the time I've spent here does make me feel as if I've somehow already been punished for my crime. Having spent nine straight hours in the dark, munching now-stale popcorn and sipping now-flat Diet Coke, watching image after image flash across the giant screen, has made me feel as if I am at the end of a middle-school sleepover or an all-nighter during college exam week.

It's not as if I've disliked this whole experience: I did feel an excited buzz each time I snuck into a forbidden theatre and a subsequent buzz each time those endless ads and previews finally ended and the opening credits rolled onto the screen. But by the middle of the second movie, I was already starting to feel like I do at one of those restaurant meals when I realize that I've ordered way too much food or one of those family reunions that has gone on two or three days too long. In other words, I was barely into my twelve-hour movie experience before I started kicking myself for overdoing it.

Poking my head out the door of theatre 13, I see that the coast looks clear—there is not an usher or theatre manager in sight. All I've got to do to pull off this five-movies-in-one-day caper is walk straight down the hall to theatre 11 where I can see the red neon sign: "Atonement . . . 9:45." But suddenly it hits me: I don't think I can stand sitting through one more minute of one more movie. In fact, I'd give anything to get out of this megaplex immediately, out into the cold air. The only thing keeping me here is that I told myself—and my wife and my brother and a few of my friends—that I was going to do this, that I was going to see five movies, that I was going to stay in a multiplex from noon to midnight. And so now I feel I must see it through to the bitter end.

But wait: if staying is an act of obligation, if staying is the thing that others now expect of me and that I now expect of myself, then wouldn't leaving now be an act of defiance, a way to demonstrate that I don't always give in to a need to live up to the expectations that I've set up for myself? Wouldn't walking out right now be a spontaneous act? What would I prove by sitting through two hours and three minutes of *Atonement*? That I can stick to a schedule? That I can stay out and stay up till midnight?

Actually I'm not at all sure that I *can* stay up till midnight: I'm exhausted. And that's probably the least of my physical problems: after nine popcorn-filled hours of movie-watching, my back is killing me, my stomach feels queasy, and my eyes, I can tell, are getting puffy and bloodshot. Okay; that's enough: I'm making a break for it.

Stepping out into the concourse, I suddenly see, to my horror, that the bright blue sports-coat-wearing, ear-plugged, mouth-pieced, assistant manager is walking briskly and purposely right toward me. Damn. But almost immediately I see two other things: first, that this assistant manager is Bonnie what's-her-name, a twenty-something kid that one of my daughters went to school with years ago and, second, that she is not rushing toward me but right past me down the hall, apparently on an emergency mission to turn up the volume or turn down the temperature in theatre 15.

To my left I see the side exit door, leading directly into the parking lot. But I turn right instead, walk past *Atonement*, and head toward the lobby, suddenly feeling an urge to go out the way I came in, to see this thing through in dramatic fashion. When I hit the lobby, I could be thinking about how sneaking into movies is not exactly a profile in courage or the stuff of high drama. I could be thinking about how old or sore or tired I'm feeling. Or about how the people that I'm feeling so brave walking past—the ushers, the ticket taker, the candy sellers, the manager in the glass booth—are definitely not the same people I walked past at noon. But instead, I suddenly feel lighter than I have for hours, more alert and alive. I am a cool-as-smoke mastermind who has just pulled off the perfect crime—I'm George Clooney in *Oceans 11* or Kevin Spacey in *The Usual Suspects*—and I am now walking, unrecognized and unflappable, right past all the clueless people who have absolutely no idea that anything remarkable is happening.

"Hep"
Mary Pinard

Mary Pinard is a poet and Associate Professor of English at Babson College where she teaches literature and poetry writing courses in the Arts and Humanities Division. Since coming to Babson in 1994, she has directed the Rhetoric Program, coordinated the Writing Center, and served as division chair. Her poems have appeared in numerous journals and she won first prize for single poems in the Emily Dickinson and The Nebraska Review poetry contests. She was born and raised in Seattle. And whenever she can, she flies.

> Air an instrument of the tongue,
> The tongue an instrument
> Of the body. The body
> An instrument of spirit,
> The spirit a being of the air.
>
> —Robert Pinsky

t was probably in spring, 1962, when I first saw her. It would have been in the slightly dim den of our house in Seattle, where my recently widowed father and I spent almost every Sunday night watching *The Ed Sullivan Show* on TV. It would have been grainy through the glow of black and white, but in my memory, the woman on the flying trapeze was a jeweled bird: rare, daring, free.

Rapt, I watched her—raven-black hair loose down her back, her body glittering in sequin flashes as she grasped the slim bar, then on tiptoes leaping off the high and impossibly tiny platform, swinging into a graceful arc across the netless stage, and then somehow, while swinging, she shifted her position to dangle from her knees, still swinging, and she reached her long arms up, her back arching until she reached for a thin but muscular man in a leotard swinging even higher who, from his own bar and upside down, caught her by her wrists, drawing her easily off her bar, and together, they then swung, like some long human necklace undone, through the air, back, and then, in the middle and in midair, he let her go, lifting her up just slightly as he did to start her whirling through a half turn in perfect time for her to meet her own bar again, appearing from nowhere it seemed, and just under her fingers, which she simply hooked over the bar, and continued, swinging from it back to the tiny platform that only came once again into view as her pointed toes touched it, and while the rest of her body followed, she let the bar swing empty behind her, and she turned to face us, smiling, so beautiful, holding up one arm, waving.

I was five at the time, and like most kids, I'd been asked by adults, "What do you want to be when you grow up?" Though I'd never had a ready answer—one knows everything and nothing at the age of five—once I'd seen the flying trapeze artist on TV, I knew my answer. But it would be over forty years before I ever said it out loud to anyone, or gave it a try.

The word *trapeze* originates with the Greek *trapezion*, which literally means small table, and happens to describe quite accurately the quadrilateral shape formed by a crane bar and a trapeze bar across the shorter ends, and the two linking lines along the longer sides. While our contemporary sense of the circus wouldn't be complete without a trapeze act, the first trapeze wasn't invented until 1859, when, for twelve breathtaking minutes and without falling through the net-free air of the Cirque Napoleon in Paris, Jules Léotard, age twenty-one, performed on a rig featuring three trapezes. Swinging and leaping from one to the next, and at some point successfully completing the first midair flying trapeze somersault, Léotard found that his long, lonely practices had paid off. Bored with what his father's rather conventional gymnasium had to offer—his father taught gymnastics for a living—Léotard had for some time retreated to the swimming pool, where he suspended a horizontal bar from some ventilator cords and set to work to perfect his aerial tricks (and their inverse, falling) above and into the water. When he transferred these release and flight patterns to larger, less watery performance spaces, he placed a series of mattresses on a raised runway to offer his audiences a better view (Kissell).

Léotard also found incredible fame. He became one of the world's first superstars, appearing over the next ten years or so in several European capitals, as well as in the United States, until his untimely death in 1870, apparently from small pox (Bolton). According to an eyewitness account of one of Léotard's performances by G. Strehly, author of *L'Acrobatie et les acrobates*,

> This "saltimbanque" was the king of fashion. It's hard to believe the welcome he received in Paris. When there is not much politics, the public's passion looks for an object. For a while, Léotard was that object. He caused a storm everywhere. There were queues to get into the Circus; people fought for seats. In addition, advertising assured that the artist's name was in vogue, and we saw the appearance of Léotard cravats, Léotard walking sticks, Léotard brooches. (qtd. in Bolton)

King of fashion indeed. If that name, *Léotard*, puts you in mind of lithe musculature and ease of motion for limb and torso, you'll understand now since there's a reason. As if it weren't enough to invent the apparatus and its artful tricks, Léotard also designed the skintight, one-piece garment, that marvel of functionality and flair that bears his name and has become synonymous with the practice of acrobatics and dance.

And isn't it a kind of second skin for flyers? The merest, modest cover, and at the same time, the boldest pronouncement of those shapely limbs, the thick torso, a ribbed purse for the heart? That we have over the decades, since its first appearance on its creator's frame, encumbered and encrusted it with all manner of feathers, rhinestones, metallic threads and wire, invisible seams, rickrack, rip-stop, and Velcro fasteners, suggests perhaps that we want to elevate those who wear the leotard to the status of birds, or even angels—in any case, we desire a being possessed of a fragile beauty but inspired by a strong heart and pure courage. Someone who dazzles us with daring.

Ever since I can remember, I wanted to fly. And not with the help of anything mechanical or pharmaceutical—I wanted my *body*, on its own, to fly. I understood very early on that this presented certain obstacles, and I began to imagine ways to overcome them. I also understood that these flights of fancy were better kept to myself— there was no telling what kinds of limits the adults in my life might impose on me should they ever discover what, literally, I had going through my mind. They always seemed to have visions of potential danger going through theirs. But there was also for me a kind of delight, a delicious mischief in holding back my dangerous wish to make and take flight: by keeping it entirely to myself, it became entirely mine. I had complete control over its design, its rules, its costumes, its physics, its destiny: in a word I was its creator. And perhaps this was my first experience with art, if art is in fact the expression of what is beautiful, or at least of something with more than ordinary significance.

Regardless, I spent considerable time practicing in my backyard some of the skills that made sense for someone who wanted to fly— knee hanging, flipping, and swinging—on a set of rusting jungle gym bars equipped with one worn wooden swing. I set mostly impossible goals for myself, always pushing to achieve the longest dangle (preparation for vertigo and varieties of dizziness, but also an effort to test whether my so-called rib cage could potentially unlock itself and if so, what might that feel like); the most consecutive revolutions starting from a sitting straddle on top of the bar (I called these "pancakes" and considered mastery of momentum their most significant result); and the highest possible arc for seated swings. In the case of swinging, for example, the idea was to pump forward (swing back), pump forward (swing farther back), and pump pumping pumping pumppump-pump high enough so I could swing, still seated, all the way over the top of the horizontal bar, my long hair drawing a wavy but perfect circle behind me. Success in this case eluded me, but I was undeterred. I pursued other flight preparation endeavors.

I took to watching birds, perhaps the first teachers I chose on my own for my own purposes, since they appeared to have perfected not only the act of flying, but also varieties of plumage and posture to accent it aptly. Plus, birds were plentiful in my yard, especially robins. I must note too that at the time there was a cartoon show I loved on TV called *Heckle and Jeckle*, which featured two wise-cracking magpies who were wilier, brainier, and funnier than anyone in their animated world (or my real world, for that matter); they were also expert flyers and could banter with the greatest of ease, even while on the wing. I suspect it grew from some combination of the real and the cartoon, that first image I created of myself as a flyer: it took shape as a small but sturdy reddish-feathered bird, not much taller than my five-year-old self, and with a compact suitcase packed with a few provisions and hooked under the flexible tip of my right wing. When the time was right—and that meant a cloudless sunny day, not anything very usual in Seattle—I would look up, bend my skinny bird knees, and take flight with no effort or fear or regret. In my mind's eye, I watched myself from the ground as my ever-shrinking figure wing-flapped up and up and away, my threadlike claws dangling, and finally disappearing into the deep blue sky. Why did I want to fly? And where did I think I was going, or what, to ask it another way, was I leaving?

Some who have never flown on a trapeze—or even *thought* about it—might assume that those who do are either professional circus performers, or simply daft, attention-seeking daredevils motivated by bravado, impetuous folly, or even an unconscious death wish. Why else would anyone *choose* to do something so perilous, maybe even crazy? There have been studies conducted, especially in the areas of personality research and anthropology, to explore why people take

dangerous chances. Lisa Hofsess, an ex-professional aerialist and college professor, completed psychological research into trapeze artists
and risk-taking for her degree in kinesiology at Iowa State University
in 1984. Hofsess found her subjects among the Denver Imperial
Flyers, one of the oldest continually operating trapeze groups in the
world. For her control group, Hofsess used a YMCA aerobic exercise
class. After administering a battery of tests and interviews to both
groups, her results revealed that nonflyers are different from flyers.
Flyers expressed that being out of control, disoriented, and dizzy were
unpleasant feelings that they did not seek or enjoy. While they wanted
to be at the physical limits of what their bodies could do, they were
not interested in putting themselves in danger or taking unsafe risks
(Barbour 6). In fact, their main goal was mastery, a sense of accom-
plishment or challenge, not only in terms of the immediate environment—the trapeze, the rig from which it is suspended, and the
net—but also in terms of unrelated events.

In addition to mastery, members of the Denver Imperial Flyers
reported that they experienced deep excitement while flying and
appreciated the aesthetic beauty of the motion and movement it
entails. I was particularly interested in what Hofsess wrote in her
study about the flyers' responses when asked what they would miss
the most if they were no longer able to fly. Most said it would be the
social interaction. From spending time with a group of flyers, even if
they came from very different backgrounds and circumstances, or
only met to fly together, they felt mutual respect, affection, and trust.
Some even spoke of the ways in which flying and the control and
calm it required them to practice and master helped them gain satisfaction and self-esteem. Hofsess reports:

> Within the course of the interviews, which focused on cognitive
> and affective processes during flying, several flyers volunteered
> details of traumatic personal incidents including rape, parental
> abuse, and severe physical injury, most commonly from automo-
> bile accidents. Without exception, and without prompting, they
> claimed that their involvement within the emotionally support-
> ive atmosphere of flying facilitated psychological management of
> the (psychological) injury caused by the reported trauma. (16)

Apparently, the flyers also made frequent references to "family" in describing their closeness with one another, and one flyer offered that maybe they should wear feathers (Barbour 6).

For my forty-seventh birthday in 2003, my stepdaughter gave me a certificate for one flying trapeze lesson on an outdoor rig along the Hudson River in New York City. I was thrilled and grateful, but also completely flabbergasted. "How did you know I wanted to fly on a trapeze?" I asked. She looked at me with disbelief—it felt a little searing actually—then shook her head slowly, saying with a hint of skepticism, "You've only been talking about it for *years*. How could I *not* know?" I was pretty sure that I'd gotten over my youthful determination to keep most things that I considered important to myself, which mostly meant hidden from adults. But I guess on some level I must have believed that my "secret" wish to fly had stayed tucked away deep inside. Here, though, was evidence that it hadn't, and in the shape of a gift certificate for a flying trapeze lesson. I must not have been able finally to hold my secret secret. Without my actually realizing it, I had not only given it words—*I want to fly, I want to fly on a trapeze*— but I had said it out loud, and in the presence of my stepdaughter. What else could I do but schedule a lesson?

The act of flying on a trapeze is, like so many artful activities, much harder than it looks. Part of its art is making it look easy. Part of its art is its discipline, its exacting and precise use of the human body to create fluidity and the illusion of weightlessness and flight. When I first saw the female flying trapeze artist on TV, I thought she *was* flying—it was that suggestive of the real thing. What I've understood by attempting to fly on a trapeze myself is how its fluidity depends on particular physical skills, precise timing, exacting focus, and sustained courage and calm. There is also considerable pain involved in this art—hands blistered and ripped, calves seared by net burns, fingers dislocated, muscles torqued—not to mention the discomforts more specific to an older flyer, like embarrassment at failing a trick, or regret due to a permanently inflexible hip, or the fallibility attendant with the loss of stamina.

When I went for my first lesson, it was a perfect spring day in New York City—cloudless cornflower-blue sky, just enough sun to warm my face, hands, and feet (the only bare skin showing beyond the delicate neck, sleeve, and ankle hems of my leotard), and a slight breeze off the water. The outdoor rig at the Trapeze School New York is situated along the Hudson River, just about at Canal Street, so flyers have a great view of the surrounding sites, and those out for a walk along the river have an equally great view of the flyers: thus regardless of your level of skill or experience, you are bound to have an audience. Everyone receives basic information about correct positioning for the body, especially the shoulders, arms, and feet, as well as safety training. I remember feeling astonished at how brief this portion of the lesson was; I hadn't been there twenty minutes before I was climbing the twenty-four-foot metal ladder to the impossibly tiny platform, a safety belt cinched around my waist, and chalk dust keeping my palms dry, at least for the moment.

I don't remember exactly the last time I saw my mother, but there is somewhere inside me the mark of memory that tells me that the last thing I saw her *do* was wave to me. It was clearly a moment of departure, but not one that I, or anyone else at the time, could have recognized as so very final. She and my father left for a vacation trip by car to southern California in early February 1962, leaving my three older brothers, myself, and my younger sister at home with our great-aunts, Alice and Estelle. We loved them, as we knew our parents did; in fact we thought of them as doting second parents. It wasn't until many years later that I learned how accurate an appellation that was since they had acted as "parents" for my mother when her parents died by the time she was nine, leaving her an orphan in their care. When she turned ten, they brought her to Seattle from where she had been living in a small town in Minnesota, and she started a new life as a niece. Alice and Estelle were nimble in the midst of loss, accustomed to filling at least some of the gaps left in its wake.

So when the phone rang at our house in Seattle on that wintry day in late February with news that my parents had been in a serious car accident in Bakersfield, California, just at the start of their journey home, my great-aunts were stoic. But not for long. When they learned that their niece had in fact been killed in the wreck, and her husband seriously injured, they wept, and I wept to see their tears, though not because I knew the truth. In fact, years would pass before anyone told me the details of my mother's death earlier that day, how she had been thrown from the car, literally flown out of it as it flipped over and over in air, and how she was found in the end, underneath it, mortally injured. Instead of explaining the situation to me and preparing me for its long, long result, however, my great-aunts made up stories.

"Oh, she's not coming home for now."

"Well, when will she be home?"

"Oh, we're not sure, but you'll see her eventually."

"Well, where will I see her?"

"Oh, look in this holy book, the one that shows us God and all his heavens—see this picture of a line of beautiful angels, singing? That's where your mother is, what she's doing, and that's where she'll be, for a while anyway."

I have a distinct memory of scrutinizing this picture, trying to find, then to imagine, my mother among this line of female strangers dressed in shapeless white robes. I recall what might have then been my first experience of skepticism as I noted that all these so-called angels were blond, and I knew my mother's hair was as black as a raven's.

After that day, everything turned, and turned upside down. And all that kept me focused was waiting for my missing mother to return: hours sitting at the downstairs picture window that faced the street, hours watching, hours listening for a key in the door, hours wandering around my yard checking for traces of her, hours, like some detective, spying on anyone who even slightly resembled my mother, then hours more spying on anyone who *didn't* resemble my vanished mother, since who knew? She could be a runaway, escapee, fugitive, hiding, wearing a disguise, maybe, maybe because she'd decided she didn't *want* to come home, maybe because she'd decided her children were bad, or maybe it was just her first daughter who was bad, who was to blame, that mischievous girl, that daredevil of the bars, high-swinging, knee-scraping tomboy, that first daughter, that bad, bad girl. Maybe it was only me keeping her away. Over time I got good at filling in the huge space that was her absence with explanations, stories full of sad, sad endings, and occasionally, a scrap of a small story of hope: there was still that flying going on in my head, that leap into freedom, that rush of air around my ears, all waiting ended, all weight suspended as I let go, turn and rotate, wing myself home to safety. There was, at least, that.

Of course Alice and Estelle, and many good family friends and neighbors were present during this time, doing what they could to help out, offer support, get us through, somehow. But no one's body was my mother's body, no one's.

The body, the platform, the head held up, eyes fixed forward, the trapeze, the chalked hands hooked around it, the shoulders held in their sockets, the slight leap up, toes pointed, legs held together, the downward drop, the start of the swing across, then knees up and over the bar, hands off, body penduluming back toward the platform and forth again, hands up, hook the bar, knees off, full body dangling for one more swing, back and forth, then lifting the legs, now in a sitting position in flight, let go, still holding the position, and drop, down, down, land in the net, bounce up, land again, seeing the sky through the high silver guy wires.

So much about flying is physical: that solid act involving the flesh, blood, and boney body. And yet it can only happen in or through a medium, that is, nonetheless, less, a space that is, frankly, nothing: that formless, simply everywhere and nowhere presence we call air. Air. Atmosphere maker, a mix of gases, a stir, a look, a tune, breath: its seeming none-ness, its whoosh, its silence, its epitome of openness, its push. For me there is a lovely tension between the concrete and the abstract in flying on a trapeze: its pure embodiment expressed through its silky but surely invisible ambiance, its biological proofs lined up with its metaphysics of physics. I feel this same kind of tension when I'm writing, certainly when I work on prose, but with even more intensity when I work on making poems. That sturdy horizontal trapeze that I grasp when I fly—that solid shape I hold on to, let go, then return to, take up again—is for me like a line of poetry, that unit of urgent composition that I, as a poet, must make strong enough, true enough, concise enough to carry meaning across space. It must be just the right balance of lilt and meter, image and story to survive a leap into the sky of the empty page. Who hasn't felt the risky rush of facing that white blankness, that possibility?

Long before I ever touched a real trapeze bar and swung with it away from a platform, I was writing poetry. While I can't say for sure, I think I started making poems when I was in high school, mostly as a way of trying to give shape to deep but confused feelings I had about loss in my life. These early poems were extremely condensed and very cryptic—like small, tight word parcels tied almost shut with strict rhyme and sparse imagery, and probably not meant to be opened by anyone. I can say for sure that it was around this time that my father fell in love again, and after over ten years of being the eligible widower in our community, he announced at one Sunday breakfast at home, rather offhandedly, that he and our new stepmother had eloped three weeks earlier. My siblings and I were happy for him, of course, but we felt left out for not being included in the wedding plans, and more significantly, I think we felt the loss of our own mother all over again, and with a new kind of finality. There would be for me no more imagining my mother's body in our house, no more thinking about her as she might have been so many years later, and certainly no more waiting for her to return. How could there be if there was now a new woman, a new mother of sorts, in the house, and someone bearing no resemblance to my own? Something about the fact that my mother's physical absence so early in my life had gone unexplained meant that I had been able to imagine into the emptiness she left behind, which for me would always be defined by her image, or at least what I wanted that image to be. I could create her in my mind, again and again, and of course, revise her as I saw fit: I literally shaped her, thus bringing her to life in my mind. This practice was emotionally comforting, I'm sure, but it also engaged me in the act of making and shaping, that leap of faith, that terribly scary but satisfying thing we do when we risk expression through the use of form.

In my reading about the history of the trapeze and its invention as a form of daring circus technique, I read, of course, about the history of the circus. I thought I knew something about the ancient Roman circuses, those events involving chariot races, wrestling, and probably hungry lions, and assumed that our modern circus is derived from these early spectacles. But according to Hovey Burgess, master teacher of circus, author of *Circus Techniques*, and circus pedagogue, there is considerable confusion about where our notions of circus originate. Burgess argues that the modern circus does not descend directly from the Romans and that their circuses, "such as *Circus Maximus*, were architectural structures designed primarily for chariot races. Some confusion arises from the frequent translation of 'panem et circenses' as 'bread and circuses' when, in fact, it means 'bread and races' " (Burgess 66). He goes on to explain that the first modern circus, the New British Riding School or Amphitheatre Riding Ring, built in 1770 and designed to accommodate exhibitions of riding, clowning, vaulting, and other circus-type skills, was not called a circus either. But it did feature what has become the abiding symbol, the literal form of the circus: a ring. This form, Burgess asserts, and its exact diameter of forty-two feet, is the one element that has remained constant for circus performances: "This seems to be the diameter that creates the steadiest speed and the optimum balance between centrifugal and centripetal forces for a man attempting to maintain his balance on the back of a galloping horse" (66). Thus the limitations of the circus ring, mathematically determined and realized through a combination of human and animal skill and finesse, are like other forms that shape artful expression: the metrical patterning of a line of poetry, the ratio of feather and barb to hollow bone in the curve of a bird's wing, and the gravity and desire combined in the arc of a flyer's swing.

When I finally reached the platform at the top of the ladder, my trapeze instructor said, "Okay, you can step across." What I was stepping across was air, all twenty-four feet deep of it there between me and the ground. There was a net stretched some distance below, and there was the welcoming hand of my instructor, and with barely a pause, I took that step. Though smaller than seemed safe, the platform was remarkably sturdy, and I felt, well, at ease in this high, slightly windy, distinct space. While my instructor hooked another safety line to the carabiner dangling from my safety belt, I glanced out over the glittering Hudson River, noting a few boats chugging by, and closer in, along the asphalt path along the banks of the river, clusters of people gathered, looking up, looking, it seemed, at me. Where was I, exactly? Certainly in a place I'd never been before, but why wasn't I more afraid? Why didn't this high, rigged place feel odd, new?

Before I had time to think about it, my instructor told me step forward on the platform and line up my toes with the edge. I did, and looked over and down where I saw the net, a wide, generous weave shifting just slightly in the wind. Then with a large, long-handled hook, my instructor caught the side rope of the trapeze and pulled it toward us on the platform: "Here's your bar," he said. I leaned forward and with my right hand grabbed hold of the trapeze. It felt hard, even with the lapped layers of tape running around and around it. "And when you're ready, you can lean out and take the bar in your other hand." Leaning, and noticing that, if it weren't for my instructor's steady hand holding my belt at the back, I would have left the platform, literally tumbling off, falling, much sooner than I was supposed to. Now I had my bar, my solid line of contact which would, in a matter of moments, carry me into flight. I think I remembered to breathe, but I can't be sure. I knew I needed to listen for the word *Hep*, which in trapeze parlance signals a change and means "Go!" And before I could even wonder when, I heard it: "Hep."

And I jumped. And I flew. And it was as if I had always flown, and known this free space as home.

Since that first time in New York City, I've flown on the flying trapeze at several other rigs in Boston and Vermont, and when I can during my visits with my stepdaughter, her husband, and their daughters, I return to the outdoor rig along the river. It's hard for me to believe sometimes that I didn't actually fly until I was forty-seven years old, since even the first time I did it, I felt completely comfortable, whole, completed somehow through the act of climbing, leaping, flying, and falling into the net. How could something I'd never done be that easy? I've understood, of course, that it wasn't really the first time. I'd been taking flight in my mind since what really was my first time, when I was five and watching my jeweled bird of a trapeze artist fly across the stage on *The Ed Sullivan Show*. From that day, I was practicing my own art of flying, both those endless flight patterns in my mind as well as my other mode of flying, which is writing. I've also understood that my initial attraction to the woman on the flying trapeze was no doubt psychologically connected to the loss, just months prior, of my own mother in that violent car accident. It seems to me entirely possible that the black-haired, jeweled flyer, literally swinging into my mind's eye at almost the same moment in time when my own mother flew forever out of my view, was a form shaped by my own grief and love and need for repair. And I see now how in my life as an adult, themes of loss, risk, and willfulness in the face of emptiness (literally stepping off that platform into open air) intertwine with and emerge through my explorations of the flying trapeze.

Even that image of the robin I chose for myself when I needed both to escape the loss I sensed and to grasp the power of my own will to ascend and find freedom—that solitary flyer with the reddish plumage and one small suitcase packed for travel—seems inspired by my first woman on the flying trapeze. The scientific name for the robin, which is a kind of thrush known for its tuneful song, is from the Latin, *Turdus migratorious*, and means to be migratory, a wanderer. I have also read that during nest-building, the female robin may have mud streaked across her breast due to pressing it against the muddy lining as she forms the inner cup of the home she builds for her nestlings (Stokes 340). I like knowing that this migratory singer, this feathered spirit is also marked by the earth and her most meaningful inhabitants. It makes me proud to be a fellow flyer, a form, a being of the air.

Note

The epigraph is taken from "Song," a poem by Robert Pinsky written especially for inclusion in *A Convergence of Birds: Original Fiction and Poetry Inspired by the Work of Joseph Cornell* (2001) edited by Jonathan Safran Foer. Here is the poem in its entirety.

Song

Air an instrument of the tongue,
The tongue an instrument
Of the body. The body
An instrument of spirit,
The spirit a being of the air.

The bird a medium of song.
Song a microcosm, a containment
Like the fresh hotel room, ready
For each new visitor to inherit
A little world of time there.

In the Cornell box, among
Ephemera as its element,
The preserved bird—a study
In spontaneous elegy, the parrot
Art, mortal in its cornered sphere.

Works Cited

Barbour, Allan. "History of the Denver Imperial Flyers." Winter 2006. <http://www.damnhot.com/trapeze/Imperial/HISTORY%20OF% 20THE%20 DENVER%20IMPERIAL%20FLYERS-2.htm>.

Bolton, Reginald. "The Philosopher on the Flying Trapeze: Lyotard or Leotard?" *Discourse: Interdisciplinary Journal of Philosophy.* 2003. <http://www.usfca.edu/philosophy/discourse/9/bolton.pdf>.

Burgess, Hovey. "The Classification of Circus Techniques." *The Drama Review* 18.1. (1974): 65–70.

Hofsess, Lisa. "Those Daring Young Men (and Women) on the Flying Trapeze: Impetuous Folly or Calculated Mastery?" *The Association for the Anthropological Study of Play Newsletter* 12.2 (1986): 14–17.

Kissell, Joe. "The Trapeze: How Jules Léotard Revolutionized the Circus." 12 Nov. 2004. <http://itotd.com/articles/366/the-trapeze>.

Stokes, Donald and Lillian. *Stokes Field Guide to Birds: Eastern Region.* Boston: Little Brown and Company, 1996.

Surfacing: Secrets of the Women's Locker Room

Lynn Z. Bloom

Lynn Z. Bloom is Board of Trustees Distinguished Professor and Aetna Chair of Writing at the University of Connecticut. She learned the essentials of writing from Dr. Seuss, fun; Strunk and E. B. White, elegant simplicity; Art Eastman, nitpicking revision; and Benjamin Spock, precision. These precepts govern her teaching and inform the heart, soul, and human voice of her writing, including essays collected in Composition Studies as a Creative Art *(1998),* The Seven Deadly Virtues and Other Lively Essays *(2008),*

and Writers Without Borders *(2008). "(Im)Patient"—the story of two rotator cuff surgeries necessitated by her daily swims over thirty years— was named a Notable Essay of 2005. She still swims every day.*

Every day, year round, I swim laps. After a dozen years at the university pool, most of the regulars, including faculty, even some students, migrated three years ago to the newly opened community recreation center. The parking is close at hand; no more lugging gym bags across campus. With its reliable staff, we no longer mill about in damp towels, shivering in wait for the no-show guard. The water in the regulation pool (the rec center modestly refrains from bragging "Olympic-sized," though that's what it is) seems slightly warmer than the university's. There's a smaller pool with designated hours for rehab, and other times for families (our infant grandson was initiated on a recent visit)—invited to play with rubber duckies, frogs, and best of all, spouting whales. I have read in the *New York Times* about gyms, even the swanky ones, where vigilant attendants have to keep people from hogging the exercise machines, fighting over the lap lanes, and commandeering all the locker space, but except for a few children who evade parental discipline, this is not the local ethos. The lobby offers magazines (bring some from home, take what you want), Internet connections, free coffee. The perfect setting for conversation. But the locker room is better, especially since it has been designated a "cell phone–free zone."

When I was new to the campus, all the bodies were blurred, streaked figures in or out of water in the pool and in the university's common shower room, suitable for George Bellows' boxers with its harsh lights, sweating pipes, cracked tiles, concrete floor, no curtains. Politeness dictated no staring, though it was hard to ignore the presence of people who appeared naked inches away under the shower day after day. In those days I would silently compare my body to theirs. Fatter than me. Thinner. Breasts bigger than mine, they could scarcely be smaller. Is she pregnant, or just flabby? Older than me. Younger. The spraying water bestowed innocence, washing away makeup, hairdos, neutralizing skin colors.

We moved in concert when the toilets were flushed in the adjacent room, dance or be scalded. Gradually we began to talk, under the streaming water. Where to get good maple syrup. Sightings of blue-birds, coyotes, a red fox. Hiking and youth hostelling in Australia's Blue Mountains, and Tasmania. Peace Corps work in the Peruvian Andes. RN training in hospitals versus college nursing programs. When to plant tomatoes so they wouldn't freeze. How children learn three foreign languages simultaneously, with native accents, and never mix them up. The Met's pre-Impressionism show ("Don't go"). Dissertation research—astrophysics, patiently explained, and explained again . . . . Sometimes we talked when we swam laps, with pauses for the turns—as we do in the new pool.

The new community building has separate shower stalls, but we continue to dress in a common area, now Mondrian in functional design but populated with bodies by Rubens, Renoir, Picasso (in all incarnations—rose, blue, cubist), Jacob Lawrence, Frida Kahlo, anime. The conversation continues, the reclusive hiding beneath headphones, iPods, big towels. A Mexican linguist knows good places to learn Spanish, "But it's really easy anywhere with an inter-active computer program." What and where to feed horses during a summer of drought. How to encourage more girls to study science. Could they be recruited through UConn's summer program for kids, in which last summer's physics class consisted of twenty boys—and one girl who dropped out when she saw the numbers. An AAUW activist is on the case. Good books to read. Book club choices, pro and con.

When we're discussing the ambivalent mother of the narrator with Asperger's syndrome in *The Curious Incident of the Dog in the Night-Time*, I compliment the mother of a spastic teenage daughter on her consistent, soothing kindness. She smiles in reply, "Parents without patience don't come here." A lawyer, a divorce mediator, devours history, biography, autobiography—works that show people taking charge of their own lives. "The people I represent are so powerless. No money, no leverage, no hope of better jobs. In most cases, I hate to say, they'd be better off to stay married." "Can you tell them that?" "Not unless they ask. Their minds are usually made up by the time they see me." "Are they women?" She knows I'm an English professor, and tactfully ignores the fact that I've asked the obvious. "Every one of them." "I'll email you that autobiography reading list," I promise.

I think of this conversation when I overhear the Voice of Experience advising newly divorced Innocence on the virtues of becoming a landlady as a way to augment her income. "Buy a duplex," Experience recommends, "You can claim tax deductions not just for the mortgage, but for repairs, painting, cleaning—even the mops and cleanser. It will pay for itself in four or five years." She may be right, I think, aware that even small apartments here rent for $1300 a month. "The only trouble," says Experience, "is dealing with the tenants. But you can be very upfront in telling them what you expect. I know of a house near here that's just come on the market." As Innocence heads for the exercise room, Experience promises, "Tomorrow I'll give you a list of what not to do when you start dating again. I wish I'd figured this out the first time around, the second time—we're not married, but we're living together—is so much better."

Even on dry land we dive beneath the surface. Issues close to home. On one super hot day as we shiver in wet bathing suits in the air-conditioned dampness, I observe to a woman I've never met before, "The first thing we did when we moved here was to install central air conditioning. Some summers we hardly use it, but it keeps us up to speed on days like this." "We only have a window air conditioner in our bedroom," she moans, "And the kitchen is sweltering. We have electric heat," which means a lot of money and upheaval to install air conditioning. "I'd rather move to get air conditioning than remodel." Her face breaks into a smile. "My son moved home right after college. Now his older brother has come home, too." "How old are they?" I ask. "They're twenty-one and twenty-three, good kids, and they're saving money by living with us. But the only freedom my husband and I have ever had was the nine months when our younger son was living in the dorm his senior year." She is smiling broadly now, "I'll sell the house. That will get them out!"

At the rec center even parents of small children can find some respite by leaving them in the nursery while they exercise. During the diaper change that invariably accompanies the reunion, older children cluster around to watch the process, smugly confident in their own continence as they exclaim over the protagonist's anatomy. Sometimes the parents discuss day care, policies, and possibilities. Health care, ditto. A pharmacist says she always volunteers to work on Thanksgiving and Christmas. "And leave your family?" I inquire, since she's often there with her adolescent daughter, who sounds as sweet as she looks. "Yes. The people who come in are so lonely. They'll buy a can of nuts they don't need and talk for a half hour. All day long they appear, there's no one at home." We speculate on the eleven-day Christmas tour of the Norwegian mail-and-passenger boats through the fjords beyond the Arctic Circle in pitch-dark day and night. What lost souls book passage on this stygian voyage? Do they, like Dante's Guido, as naked spirits speak candidly to one another in this closed circuit of incandescence, flaming out against the jagged ice of bergs, mountain crags, and northern lights so far from home? I tell people whose names I do not know things I have never told my own sister, fears, frustrations, secrets bubbling to the surface.

The doctor's office-type scale is the focal point of the room, impossible to ignore. So we all weigh ourselves, averting our eyes not from the naked body on the slightly elevated platform but from the numbers on the balance beam. Who among us does not want to lose the vacation ten? The freshman fifteen? Agile high school girls shimmy into two layers of bathing suits before removing their underwear, ecdysiastic artistry that pales before the tattoos visible on women of all ages. A discreet butterfly poised on an ankle. A rosebud amidst cleavage. A directional arrow on the derriere—you go, girl! A permanent bracelet, its inky weave overlain by plastic circlets, neon pink and yellow and green. Concentration numbers still ragged, indelible on a forearm. And scars. I stare resolutely into the eyes of a friend with a mastectomy, even though it's a decade old. A newer acquaintance, whose bald head signals recent chemo, seeks advice on a literary agent for her children's stories. Will there be time enough to develop her talent. . . . She does not finish her sentence. "Try writing the stories and see what happens," I say, and give her the name of an experienced children's author.

Unlike the cramped locker room in the old building, the new locker room has ample space for wheelchairs and rehab equipment. A woman in a back brace who has progressed from a wheelchair to a walker to a cane after three months of hydrotherapy looks svelte and tanned, erect in her uniform of tights and tunic. Another, however, has become progressively more dependent on her motorized scooter and aide. Newly wed, she tells us of her trip to California to be with her three sisters for the marriage. We survey her finger—no ring; the precious circlet, too small at the ceremony, is being enlarged. Our toast is water, always water.

Together we lift from her wheelchair yet another feminist-in-arms whose daily swims transform her crippled legs to arcs of grace. When her husband's not there to share a private family changing room, she counts on the reliable regulars to slip on her panties and slacks, and slide them up. She has served as a community consultant on the construction of this new building, for handicapped shower and toilet stalls, and we acknowledge their installation—seats, grab bars, waist-high controls, adjustable shower height—as we talk about writing, hers, mine, ours. Later we turn out strong for the publication party for her book, *Body of Diminishing Motion*, and there we are, surprise! in "Legs" and "Laps" and "Morning Swim."

Into the shower's ebb and flow, the lap lanes, the new therapy pool with warm water, the women come and go. The high school swim team seniors graduate, to be replaced by the next wave, glistening in braces and matching Speedos. Gaggles of gigglers, but at least once a week someone will be crying, usually over betrayal by a friend, boy or girl. Pregnant women, suits stretched taut, more graceful now in this immersion than on dry land, in energetic preparation for new immersion. New colleagues arrive with young children who are learning to swim and waving sodden certificates to prove it. A former grad student appears; her children have metamorphosed from dipping timid toes into the water to fearless divers, in training for the swimming team. A trio of a certain age, one teaching two friends how to breathe underwater, how to do the crawl, the breast stroke—the Three Graces, surely. Another graceful swimmer, her Warsaw ghetto accent still strong after fifty-two years of marriage and life in America, disappears the week before her husband dies, spirited off to Assisted Living by her children as they decamp for Arizona. Others leave for good—new jobs, new climates, new marriages, reunion, repatriation.

But I like it fine, right here. I would not exchange these locker room experiences for a private pool. Make no mistake. Locker rooms, like other public spaces, are known by the company they keep. Those in the Japanese "country inns," what Americans might call big spa hotels, are to die for, with every amenity for bathing, shampooing, creaming, drying. The Japanese take baths—with sprayers, handheld showers, sometimes filling small wooden tubs in fountains to rinse off—before entering the communal pool. Although we did not speak the same language, in every spa in the Hakone region I found myself amidst a cordial community of women of all ages, energetically scrubbing and inviting me, with gestures and giggles, to do the same. When we were clean within an inch of our lives, they would welcome me to the nearly scalding pool, gently splashing and pouring water in a bicultural baptism; more giggles—Mary Cassatt with Asian wash. I have never felt so much at home.

The locker room in the Stockholm hostel during another vacation was, however, of a different order. With our adolescent sons tucked in bed, and my husband off to the men's shower, I headed in the opposite direction, down a long, empty corridor where the large, hand-lettered sign tacked up on the heavy door read "Damar. Women. Frauen. Dames." The doorway revealed an abyss of midnight black, dead silent, not even a faucet dripping. When I finally found the switch there leapt forth a clean, fluorescent-lighted room that could have been painted by Edward Hopper, so spare that I had to leave my clothes and towel on the narrow windowsill.

As I turned to step into the shower, a man wearing an electric blue track suit and running shoes burst from the shower stall across the aisle. I began to scream, in impeccable English, the only language I knew by instinct, "Get out!" My voice had the wrong words, the wrong language, yet as he charged toward me I added, still screaming, "You're in the women's shower." He kept on coming, his face suffused with hatred, the eyes vacant—I have never seen such blankness before or since—looming over mine. I screamed again. Then he was hitting me on the mouth, on the cheek; I could taste the salty blood as he battered my head.

Then time slowed down, inside my head, the way it does when you think your car is going to crash as it goes into a skid, and I could hear the voices, all mine, in cacophony. One voice, terrified, could say nothing at all. I had never been hit before in my life—how could I know what to do? The man in blue, silent, never let up. "I need to get my clothes and get out," I thought. But that would mean going past him one way to retrieve them and back again to reach the door. "I should just escape," I told myself, as the windmilling blue arms continued to pound me. "If he knocks me down on the tiles," where bare feet have no traction, "he'll kill me." Still screaming I suddenly realized, "I don't want my children to hear this," but I could not stop. I was losing my balance when the angry message came, etched in adrenaline, "I didn't ask for this, I don't deserve it, and I'm not going to take it." I pushed past him and ran naked into the hall, now full of men, milling about. Although roused from sleep, they would not cross the barrier of that sign in four languages.

My husband, still wet from his own shower, came running in response to the piercing cries, surprised to find they were mine. As Martin was covering me with his travel trench coat, my assailant emerged, saw the crowd, blinked, and retreated to the sanctuary of the locker room. He stepped out again, nonchalantly, as Martin began to guide me back to our room, and this time the other men nailed him to the corridor wall and called the police. We spent much of the night at the police station filing a complaint, calling the American embassy. ("If he'd murdered you, the allegation would stand a chance," the sympathetic lawyer advised, "but Swedish law favors the criminal.") Our children slept soundly, and in the morning we continued our travels.

Although in the defiant spirit of "take back the night" I deliberately do not dwell on this story or the stories it embeds, I always feel Emily Dickinson's "zero at the bone" when I enter any locker room and it's empty. I take a sharp breath. I pause and check to see whether there are any shoes visible below the stall doors though today's unisex clothing offers ambiguous reassurance, at best. I breathe deeply. Then I plunge in anyway.

But I'm happiest when the room is crowded, a cocktail-party atmosphere with water the beverage of choice, the talking nonstop, energy level to match. This community is as fluid as the medium we swim through, life's lap lanes restorative and resilient. Over the years I've met and made good friends. A fiber artist designs and makes me the perfect dress, simple, comfortable, distinctive—"I've never done this for anyone before." An intrepid trekker and world-class photographer tells me how to arrange to walk New Zealand's Milford Track, or—if I prefer—to be dropped into northern British Columbia for wilderness canoeing, from which she has just returned, unusually fatigued by the arduous portaging of canoe-cum-tent-cum photo-graphic gear.[1] I respond with an account of our three-generational hikes in five national parks of the Canadian Rockies, the best ones followed by a swim in a pool that must close, by Canadian law the sign says, when the temperature reaches twenty-two (centigrade) below zero. I give another swimmer, a Thai microbiologist who moonlights as a caterer, copies of my books. We share recipes. We will cook together soon, in her house and mine.

When any one of us arrives, we join in the dialogue; no matter who stays or goes, the conversation carries on. The rec center's logo captures this continuity. Three bare figures, heads erect, arms and legs outstretched, on the move, are leaping in energetic silhouette against a dark circle. The largest body leads the way, bursting out on the left; the middle-sized figure is completely centered in the circle; the smallest enters from the right. The water, too, embraces all as we plunge in, move through, at our own speed, closing over each as we leave, surfacing—ever hospitable, ever open.

---

[1]The fatigue, alas, was caused not by exertion, but by invasive cancer—insidious secret, which, as her grieving husband said, "claimed her body but not her spirit," too sudden, too soon. This essay is dedicated to the memory of Carolanne Moore Markowitz.

Leaving Home

Jenny Spinner

Jenny Spinner is Assistant Professor of English at Saint Joseph's University in Philadelphia where she teaches writing and journalism and keeps an eye out for homesick freshmen in her first-year writing classes. She and her twin sister Jackie Spinner recently coauthored a memoir, Tell Them I Didn't Cry: A Journalist's Story of Joy, Loss and Survival in Iraq. Jenny Spinner lives in Drexel Hill, Pennsylvania, where she plans to stay for at least the next fifty years. Her children are welcome to stay as long as they need to.

am a college dropout. Or I was. Now I am an English professor. My students imagine a smoother sail for me into this profession of dependable dowdies. So did my parents and grandparents, my siblings, and the students and teachers of Stephen Decatur High School where I graduated in 1988 as salutatorian and poster child for overachievement. In my senior high school portrait, I'm all hair spray and brown bangs, glowing in the photographer's trick light. Against the royal blue backdrop that matches the stripes in my oversized sweater, my skin is so white it looks translucent. My signature on the back of the print is that of a girl—wide, loopy, happy. At seventeen, I am still a picture of promise.

My plan was to attend Augustana College, about four hours north of my hometown of Decatur, Illinois. Augustana is located in the Quad Cities, a cluster of towns that flank the Mississippi River at the place where the nose of Iowa nuzzles the northwestern edge of Illinois. Situated in the city of Rock Island, Augustana is a small liberal arts university affiliated with the Evangelical Lutheran Church of America. I don't remember now what first drew me to Augustana or why it was the only school to which I applied as a high school senior. In fact, I had never visited the Quad Cities until my parents drove me there for a campus visit. The typical small school spiel about intimate class sizes and caring teachers likely appealed to me, as did the Lutheran roots, which I shared. Already I knew I was more of a big-fish-in-a-small-pond kind of girl. Rock Island offered some of the comforts of home without being home.

My twin sister Jackie was headed south to Southern Illinois University, and "The Spinner Twins," as we were known in high school, would soon anchor the ends of the great state of Illinois. Until much later in our lives, when my sister would go off to war as a newspaper reporter and return home someone other than herself, high school was the most difficult period of our shared lives. We struggled those four years to figure out who we were as individuals rather than accept, as others did, the package deal the Spinner Twins offered. It's hard to be yourself, though, when someone who looks just like you shadows your every move. In high school, we shared clothes, classes, extracurricular activities, friends, and once, for a short time, a cunning boyfriend.

My sister left first. In the summer days leading to her departure, the excitement of the big transition caught hold of me, too. On occasion, I lost my breath thinking about what was to come, but the fear was only a hiccup and once I swallowed hard, it was gone. All of my friends were headed off to college, as was my twin. College wasn't a choice as much as an inevitability, and the ordinariness of the step among those around me normalized it, minimized it, even. I didn't allow myself to dwell on any concerns I might have had. I didn't talk about the fear that was building but that I was successfully keeping at bay. I picked up my oars and went with the flow because to do otherwise would have meant confronting a nagging fear that something was wrong with me. The day my sister left for school, I watched the family van pull out of the driveway, loaded with suitcases and plastic milk crates that contained sheets and towels and an emergency stash of microwave popcorn. I stood on the sidewalk waving, grinning, fooling, then took off running after her. I meant it as a joke, meant to make her laugh as she watched a version of herself appear in the side view mirror and chase her down the street. When the van reached the cornfields at the end of our street, it turned right, its red eyes blinking back at me. I stopped to catch my breath, to again swallow the fear, but it caught in my throat and stayed there for years.

While my sister happily settled in at Southern, my own attempt at college failed after just two weeks. Over the years, I've tried hard to forget those draining and miserable weeks. The memories that remain are fragmented stills of an edited movie scattered on the cutting room floor. In one I'm holding a smooth, leather volleyball in the gym where I'd gone for open tryouts. In another I'm standing outside the door of my dorm room, wrapped in a towel. A blue bandana hangs from the door, signaling that my roommate is occupied with her boyfriend and I should not enter. In another, I'm sitting in the sunny office of a professor, trying to forget my gloom and focus on our conversation about a pile of articles sitting in my lap. I remember telling her that I wanted to study journalism and feeling relieved when she advised me that Augustana did not offer a journalism major. I glazed over the alternatives she named. I could major in English and write for the *Observer*, the student newspaper, she told me. Instead, I lingered on the true gift she had given me: an out—a reasonable, respectable excuse to abandon ship.

After leaving my professor's office, I made one of my hourly phone calls home. Sometimes I phoned my parents, other times, my grandparents or my sister. At twenty-five cents per minute, these phone calls were an expensive luxury, and I paced myself, not wanting to dump the entire burden of my doom on any one person. I also wrote letters, several per day, connecting myself to home in the swirls of my pen. This time, I called my parents. "I can't stay," I told them. "They don't have a journalism major." After days of listening to my desperate phone calls home, it must have been clear to my family that something was wrong. Each day my despair turned more desperate. My unhappiness was unrelenting. I had been their peacemaker kid, their sunny Pollyanna. I wonder now if my parents were surprised by my inability to adjust to college. I know it surprised me. After all, I was a good student, a Golden Glove athlete, a class leader. How could college not be right for me? Or, how could I not be right for college? "Give it time," my parents counseled over the phone. "You'll be fine." The following weekend, they drove four long hours back to Rock Island in order to reassure me in person that I would survive if I just gave it a chance. In their defense, a lot was riding on my decision. I was at Augustana on a full scholarship.

As soon as my parents arrived that weekend, I began ticking away the minutes until they had to leave, so consumed by their impending departure that I was unable to appreciate the very thing I had been longing for all week. Their presence both comforted and embarrassed me. Even though I wanted them there, I felt ridiculous that I needed them. In nearby Moline, we boarded the Celebration Belle, a tall-stack luxury steamboat that looked like something out of the pages of a Mark Twain novel. More yellowed stills: the gray-green Mississippi rushing below my open window where I sat before a plate of prime rib and potatoes, my stomach too full of anxiety to make room for food; grim rows of stone block buildings set behind trees on the Rock Island Arsenal Garrison as we drifted past; my parents' strained faces, searching mine for answers, wondering aloud what people would think if I gave up and returned home. When my parents left on Sunday afternoon, I promised them I would try to make the best of it. Even as I promised, I knew I had already quit.

Several weeks after I withdrew from Augustana, I found myself back in Decatur, selling fine jewelry at a department store in the mall and reading *Sister Carrie* during my breaks, as if Theodore Dreiser could somehow redeem my failure. Perhaps, too, I was trying to set myself apart from the middle-aged women I worked with who did not have college degrees and who spent their lunch hour watching soap operas in the break room. Once, while I was arranging a tray of black pearls, my high school principal approached the counter. I crouched down behind a cash register and hid, not wanting him to see what had become of me. For Christmas that year, I used my paychecks to outfit my family in fine jewelry, glittering apologies for not living up to their expectations, or my own. I even bought a pendant for myself: a thin gold cross with fourteen specks of pale rubies.

The next semester, I tried again, this time at the University of Illinois, less than an hour from Decatur. With over forty thousand students, the U of I was so much bigger than any school I ever imagined myself in, and I struggled not to get swallowed up. I made it to the end of the semester, somehow managing As in my classes, but by midsummer, the thought of returning in the fall terrified me. The familiar dread would sneak up on me in midtask, rippling its way from my stomach to my throat until it felt like I was swallowing rocks. I never told anyone about these anxiety attacks because I didn't understand why I couldn't just talk myself out of them, or why I was having them in the first place. Clearly, some psychological defect was holding me back. What seventeen, then eighteen, then nineteen-year-old woman is that afraid of leaving home? What if I could never leave? I well understood that to see the world, which I truly wanted to do, I had to go out into it. The conflict was unbearable. So I sat at the dinner table with my parents and brother, my chest tight, my palms slick with sweat, embarrassed and silent. To make matters worse, my sister hadn't come home that summer. Instead, she stayed behind to work for the student newspaper, throwing herself into a career that already was taking shape for her. By the end of the summer, alone and consumed by dread, I couldn't stand to be in our old room anymore, so I moved into a camping trailer in my parent's driveway. Lying inside the trailer one night, listening to the crickets chirp from the marigold beds, I called my best friend Leslie, valedictorian of Stephen Decatur High School and now a happy, successful student at the University of Illinois. "I can't go back," I told her. "My sciatica is acting up, and the doctors won't let me do all that walking on such a big campus." There was a small grain of truth to my excuse: in high school, I had injured my sciatic nerve while sliding into second base during a softball game. This injury would follow me for the rest of my life, but in the years to come, when it pinched and caused me to limp, I would think not of sliding into second base but of what I told Leslie, of my embarrassment and shame.

How could I possibly tell her, or anyone, the truth? That I needed my mom and dad and my own bed in the bubble gum pink room I had shared with my sister for so many years. That I needed my grandmothers and my dog. That I needed the Dairy Queen on the corner of Pershing and Main where my little league teams always stopped for ice cream after victories. That I needed my grandfather's pork plant, next to the family bowling alley, down the street from the corn processing factory that spewed its malty stink into the air. If Tinkerbell had started her own island of Lost Girls for those who never wanted to grow up, I would have been the first inhabitant—as long as that island was somewhere in my own backyard. Away from home, I grew desperately homesick, for my family, for my twin, for my house, for my old, familiar life that I wanted to freeze in place. That life was far from perfect, but it was predictable and comfortable, and never lonely.

When I refused to return to the U of I, my parents insisted that I enroll at Millikin University, the college in my hometown, until I figured out what I wanted to do or where I wanted to go. They were weary of rescue hauls across the prairie. And my homesickness wasn't cute, not at my age. It was tiresome, and embarrassing. My father's letters from Vietnam, his pining for home and for my mother, that kind of homesickness is romantic, forgivable even, when something noble is at stake. In my family of hardworking, Protestant Germans, endurance was a sign of strength. "It's a great life if you don't weaken," my grandmother used to stay.

The summer before my senior year of college, I made my first sojourn away from home since enrolling at Millikin, traveling to England to study at Oxford University. Moments before I boarded the plane, my father grabbed my arm and squeezed me toward him. "Don't panic," he commanded, sending me off with a mantra that could also be interpreted as a warning. Don't panic—or else. My debilitating homesickness kicked in at Oxford as well, but I stayed the entire summer. The following year I left again, this time to attend graduate school at Penn State University. Again, the panic attacks I suffered during the first months I was there were wrenching. Two things pulled me through: my job and my cat. When I stepped through the classroom door, the gripping anxiety that launched me awake each morning suddenly dissipated, and for the next fifty minutes, I was consumed by the teaching of writing. When I arrived home each night, I was greeted by a black-haired runt that needed food, needed me, or she would die. It was enough to get me through one semester, then two, then a summer, until I no longer felt compelled to make the thirteen-hour drive home every few months.

At some point, I gained the confidence to be away. I suppose I also gave in to the reality that life was going to move on, with or without me. It's now been fifteen years since I've lived in Decatur. My grandparents are dead, as is my father. It's not that I've resigned myself to the inevitable suffering that constitutes life, given myself over to the traditional American *bildungsroman* that underwrites the "normal" course of things: Girl grows up, moves away to college, doesn't look back. I know there are other narratives, and the one I wrote for myself works, too. It's just taken years to get over the shame I felt about dropping out of school, about being one of those kids who didn't have the guts, or the maturity, or the strength to make it the first—or second—time around—especially when presented with so much opportunity, so much privilege to seize it. It's taken me years to face the excuses I told myself and others in order to cover for the real reasons I kept leaving school, to forgive myself for my longings, and to appreciate the gifts that came with staying home a few extra years.

Three years ago, a student in my first-year writing class stopped by during my office hours, grimly telling me that she planned to drop out. Why? I asked. There's no theatre major here, she explained, and that's what she really wanted. "Meg," I told her, "there's no one way to do this. If you don't want to be here, it's okay. But you're not the only one who feels what you're feeling." That I had learned in my years as a college writing professor, teaching and advising scores of homesick freshmen who are convinced that they are the only ones who are having difficulties adjusting to college. Meg and I circled campus, talking about her unhappiness, giving in to her homesickness. Maybe what I needed when I was at Augustana was permission to go home, to linger there a while longer, to try again later—and the reassurance that such a choice did not constitute weakness or defeat. I wanted to give Meg that permission, but she didn't need it. Three years later, she's still here.

Theories of Intelligence
Bruce Ballenger

Bruce Ballenger is Professor of English at Boise State University where he teaches courses in composition, composition theory, the essay tradition, and creative nonfiction. He's the author of seven books, including three texts in the Curious series: The Curious Researcher, The Curious Reader *(with Dr. Michelle Payne), and* The Curious Writer, *all from Longman Publishers. His most recent publication is* Crafting Truth: Short Studies in Creative Nonfiction.

At age 55, I've finally decided I'm not as dumb as I thought. This might seem a strange confession from a professor of English, a man who has spent twenty-five years making his living with his intellect, working all those years in an environment where being "smart" was a quality valued above all others. This revelation—that I'm not as dumb as I thought—is a relief, of course. More and more, I can sit in a meeting of my colleagues and feel okay when I'm unmoved to speak. It pains me less when I can't quite follow

someone's argument or sort out the arcane details of a curriculum pro-
posal. Now, more than ever before, I can stand in front of my classes
and say, without shame, "That's a good question. I don't really know
the answer."

It's quite possible—no, likely—that I'm not nearly as smart as
many of the people around me, but I've learned, at last, not to care.
Self-acceptance may simply be one of the few blessings of late middle
age. I was watching the news the other day and learned of a report on
happiness that suggested the midlife crisis was a universal phenomenon. The study, with the straightforward title "Is Well-Being U-Shaped
over the Life Cycle?" reviewed data from two million people in seventy-
two countries, and it concluded that American men are most miserable at around age fifty-two, perhaps because they have the sobering
realization that life did not unfold the way they hoped it would.
Happiness slowly returns when they "adapt to their strengths and
weaknesses, and . . . quell their infeasible aspirations" (20). It's a great
relief for me to know that things should be looking up.

I've considered this idea—that I'm really not that smart but have
finally accepted my limitations—but I'm coming around to the belief
that I'm probably smarter than I thought I was, that I was *always*
smarter than I thought I was. I'm pretty sure this is true for most people, and frankly, the ones who have always known they were really
smart—and who behave as if they are quite sure of this—are not the
kind of people I usually like very much. Yet even the self-consciously
smart people deserve our sympathy because being intelligent really,
really matters to most of us. We can live with being unattractive but
no one wants to feel dumb.

One of the most popular videos on YouTube is a clip from the Miss
Teen USA contest when during the interview segment of the program,
Caitlin Upton, the contestant from South Carolina, was asked this
question: "Recent polls have shown that a fifth of Americans can't
locate the U.S. on a world map. Why do you think this is?" Her
response was, sadly, completely incoherent, and the relentless, often
unkind ridicule Upton endured prompted her appearance on the
Today Show a few days later. "I was overwhelmed," she said. "I made
a mistake. Everyone makes mistakes. I'm human." I'm ashamed to
admit that I joined the throngs who gleefully watched the clip and

enjoyed Upton's humiliation; at the time, I told myself that my response wasn't personal—it just confirmed my belief that beauty pageants are socially bankrupt. But I know that the real reason I enjoyed it was the relief that it wasn't me up there.

The YouTube clip is now painful to watch, not only because the humor in humiliation wears off quickly, but I recognize in Caitlin Upton a phenomenon I see in myself: the sense that how we view our own intelligence is a script that others author and that we cannot revise. Researchers tell us that children typically have two theories of intelligence. Some believe that intelligence is an "uncontrollable trait," a thing they are stuck with like eye color or big ears. Others, particularly older children, believe that intelligence is "malleable," something they can alter through effort and hard work (296); I have never met any of these children but apparently they're out there.

It is a nearly inescapable fact of an American childhood that we are branded as smart, or somewhat smart, or not too smart, or even dumb. For many of us who lack faith in our own intelligence, this branding begins in school, a sad fact that researchers say is especially true of African American kids (113). I am white, but can trace my own experience with this by following the scent of old resentments, back to memories of school that never lose their bitter taste even when I try to sweeten them with humor. There was the time in the second grade when I was sent to the back of the room, to sit alone in a corner, because I couldn't remember all the months of the year. And later, in the eighth grade, I moved from green to orange in the SRA reading packet but never moved again. In those days, orangeness was a sign of mediocrity. The shame of never busting through orange to blue, the color Jeff Brickman, Mark Levy, and Betsy Cochran achieved with ease, convinced me that reading and writing were just not my thing, a feeling that was reinforced by my teacher Mrs. O'Neal who spattered my essays with red marks. From then on I hated school, and ironically, especially English (a feeling I freely shared on the inside covers of my class yearbooks). I spent my high school days languishing in "level 3" English and science classes where I joined the working-class Italian-American students from Highwood and the kids from the Army base at Fort Sheridan. We found solidarity in hating Shakespeare, lab reports, and the five paragraph theme. And we pretended to find solidarity in being dumb, though I think most of us were secretly ashamed.

In my junior year, I dated Jan, one of the "smart" kids who moved in a small herd, migrating from one AP class to another. I was awed by her intelligence, and in the twisted logic of an adolescent male, this awe translated into indifference; I pretended I didn't really care about her. Eventually, however, I found Jan's persistent kindness moving and began to write her bad poetry that she copied and bound into a book that she gave me for my birthday. For a time, I entertained the idea that I wasn't unintelligent. Not smart, exactly, not like Jan, but maybe I could hold my own in the AP crowd. Yet what I did not understand back then was that whatever small gains I was making in school could easily be undone at home.

There was never any question that I would go to college. My parents expected it, and so did I. But I knew that I was not destined to go anywhere Jan and her friends were headed—the University of Michigan, Brown, Tufts, Beloit, Kalamazoo. I applied to one school, Drake, with rolling admissions, and when I was accepted early, I excused myself from the endless senior chatter about colleges. I pretended I just didn't care. "You're selling yourself short," my father said, disappointed that I wouldn't pursue more schools. My brother—who was two years older—attended my father's alma mater, the University of Rochester, a school with high academic standards. Dad never encouraged me to apply there, confirming what I had already suspected—that I was a dimmer bulb.

My father was an intelligent man, a Rhodes scholar with an interest in British literature who worked for both Chicago and New York newspapers before the booze took him down. Nothing pleased him more than an argument. When I went to college in the early seventies it was an easier time for students to believe in values and ideas without being wounded by the charge that they were being "naïve." My idealism made me an easy target, and when the vodka kicked in, my father would pick up the scent of some belief I held with uninformed fervor and go after it. Even drunk, Dad knew what he was talking about, and with a cold, ruthless logic he would pick apart whatever passion I brought to the dinner table. I felt young, stupid, and hopelessly inadequate. Dad was not a cruel man, but what I know now is that his head may have been full but his heart was empty. His intellect was one of the last things he clung to as drink became the only way to dull some unspeakable pain; in the end, of course, even intellect succumbs.

There were moments after these arguments when I sat seething and my father would turn to me, wagging his finger. "The most important thing you can be, Bruce," he said, "is an intellectual. Live the life of the mind." Oddly enough, I have become an academic, and had he lived, my father would likely have approved. Yet the ache I feel about Dad these days is that he didn't possess the kind of knowing that might have saved him had he only valued it. One of the things my Dad's alcoholism taught me was how weak-kneed his kind of intelligence could be against the sucker punches of self-loathing. "Your Dad was just too smart for his own good," my mother would say. "Just too smart for his own good."

It took me a long time to see the truth in what my mom said. In college, I deflected the insecurity I felt about my intellect with an angry activism. I wrote self-important and smug columns for the student newspaper—a weekly feature called "In Defense of Nature"—chastising the student body for ignoring the environmental crisis. Only my friends read my rants, and they were kind about them. But I was also relatively successful in school and went on to graduate school at the University of Michigan and later the University of New Hampshire and did fine there, too. This evidence of intellect, accumulated over twelve years of college and graduate school, unfortunately had little effect on how I felt about myself. All it took was a moment when I felt stupid— moments we all have—and I was that boy at the dinner table again, unable to argue successfully with his intoxicated parent. Once I was invited to participate in a debate with a radio station representative over the FCC's Fairness Doctrine, which required TV and radio stations to air public service material. At the time, I was working as a spokesperson for a consumer group. The debate was staged in a public library before a group of elderly residents from a small Connecticut town, and the radio guy quickly stripped away the pretense that I knew what I was talking about. I slinked out of the room when it was over without speaking to anyone. On the drive home I sat tight-lipped and pale, furious with myself for being so stupid.

Theories of intelligence have evolved considerably since I was a child, a time when everyone was taking IQ tests. In the early eighties, Howard Gardener's "multiple intelligences" came as a relief to many of us whose scores on intelligence tests were not worth bragging about. Back then, I never really understood Gardener's theory but seized on the idea that being smart didn't necessarily mean being smart in one way. Yet I always sensed that, no matter what Gardener said, there was a kind of intelligence that really counted and that I didn't possess. It was school smarts—the ability to pick apart an argument, to recognize the logical fallacy, and to make an arresting point—all of the things, I see now, that my father could do so well. As an academic, I see these qualities in some of my colleagues, something I admire and envy. A very few of them, however, use their intelligence to bully people like my father bullied me.

Before I entered the profession, I imagined that many professors were like these intellectual bullies, people who bludgeon others with reason, looking to wound rather than to enlighten. The literary critic Jane Tompkins once wrote that college teachers are often driven by fear, "fear of being shown up for what you are: a fraud, stupid, ignorant, a clod, a dolt, a sap, a weakling, someone who can't cut the mustard" (654), and this is what drives us to do everything we can to prove to our students and others that we're intellectually superior. In rare cases, this fear of being found out turns teachers into intellectual bullies. More often, their anxiety in the classroom leads to what Tompkins calls the "performance model" of instruction: teachers talking *at* their students, teachers trying desperately to demonstrate how smart they are. It probably is no surprise that this tendency moves easily from the classroom to the department faculty meeting where the stakes feel higher.

I can't recall how exactly things began to change for me, when I started to see that I might revise the script that had governed my life for so long, but I started to notice it in those department meetings. Whether I spoke or not ceased to matter. I didn't decide one day that I was just as smart as my colleagues. I didn't suddenly start believing the strong evidence that I must have some intellectual ability since I enjoyed a successful career as a college professor. There was no sudden epiphany or dramatic moment. I think I just stopped being afraid.

It has helped to know, too, that my own ideas about intelligence don't travel well. In a famous study, developmental psychologist Joseph Glick asked a Liberian Kpelle tribesman to sort twenty items— food, tools, and cooking utensils—in a way that made "sense" to him. He did this quickly enough, pairing a knife with an orange, a potato with a hoe, and other matches that reflected the practical, functional relationships between the items. "This is what a wise man would do," said the tribesman. The researchers then asked, "What would a fool do?" The Liberian then sorted the items in what we would consider "logical" categories, putting food in one pile, cooking utensils in another, tools in another, and so on (84–87). I live a world away, of course, where as I write this my wife, Karen, is putting away the groceries using a logic that a Kpelle tribesman might find curious. The definition of a fool, obviously, depends on who and where you are.

My self-doubts will never go away completely, but I think they have made me a better teacher. I have empathy for my own students in whom I see the same struggle. Just the other night, in a graduate seminar, Greg, a particularly bright student, derailed himself in mid-sentence while interpreting a passage from a Montaigne essay we were reading. "My head just isn't working tonight," he said. "I don't know what's wrong with me." I reassured him that he was making perfect sense, but for the rest of the class Greg was solemn, his hand fixed on his forehead concealing a brow darkened by frustration. Ironically, Montaigne, a sixteenth-century philosopher and father of the personal essay, constantly questioned his own intelligence, and in the piece we were reading that night Montaigne writes that his "mind is lazy and not keen; it can not pierce the least cloud" (213). And yet, Montaigne's work celebrated his shortcomings as well as his strengths, the very things that make us human. Learning's highest calling, he thought, was to know oneself, and the essay seemed the best vessel into which this self-reflection might be poured, as I have done here.

On the advice of a friend, I recently took up meditation, a practice that often involves visualization. Sometimes as I listen to the slow rhythm of my breathing there are moments when I meet myself on a beach on Nantucket Island, a place I spent a spring nearly thirty years ago. There are just the two of us there, one young with a navy blue beret and his hands thrust in the pockets of his khaki pants, and the

other the grayer, bearded man I see in the mirror these days. I am
walking with that younger self on the empty beach at sunset, and I
have my arm around his shoulders. I am whispering something to
him meant to be comforting. I might be saying many things, but lately
I imagine it is this: "You're going to be okay." I think that learning to
fully believe this will be the smartest thing I'll ever do.

Works Cited

Aronson, Joshua, Carrie B. Fried, and Catherine Good. "Reducing the
Effects of Stereotype Threat on African American College Students
by Shaping Theories of Intelligence." *Journal of Experimental
Psychology* 38.2 (2002): 113–25.

Blanchflower, David G., and Andrew J. Oswald. "Is Well-Being U-
Shaped over the Life Cycle?" National Bureau of Economic
Research Working Papers no. 12935, Cambridge, MA, 2007.

Cole, Michael, John Gay, Joseph A. Glick, and Donald W. Sharp. *The
Cultural Context of Learning and Thinking.* New York: Basic Books,
1971.

Kinlaw, Ryan C., and Beth Kutz-Costes. "Children's Theories of
Intelligence: Beliefs, Goals, and Motivation in the Elementary
Years." *Journal of General Psychology* 34.3 (2007): 295–311.

Montaigne, Michel de. *Essays.* Trans. J. M. Cohen. London: Penguin,
1958.

Tompkins, Jane. "Pedagogy of the Distressed." *College English* 52.6
(October): 653–60.

E-Love

Harriet Malinowitz

Harriet Malinowitz is Professor of English at Long Island University, Brooklyn, and commutes there from her upstate Hudson River Valley town of Kingston, New York. She teaches creative nonfiction (and many other things) as well as first-year composition and has published fiction, journalism, theatre and book reviews, personal essays, stand-up comedy, and a play as well as academic scholarship. She is also an activist, hiker, serious talker, lover of old houses, and time waster.

The world is much more enthusiastic about art than it is about artists. A tortured painting can be revered, but a tortured painter is nervously avoided. A wildly exuberant symphony receives a standing ovation while its wildly exuberant composer gets treated for bipolar disorder. A fine piece of critical writing is lauded, but the obsessively observant person who produced it is more likely to be called a critical bitch.

The urge to write always struck me with the bludgeoning insistence of a biological drive, but this didn't make me a "writer"; it just made me a vaguely strange child. I spent many hours alone in my attic bedroom writing unfinished prose pieces that I stuffed into a drawer, believing that this was one of those things that everyone secretly did but nobody talked about. At home in Queens, I was regarded as voluble and judgmental (presumably without an inner life); at school, I was spaced out and barely noticed (with nothing, presumably, *but* an inner life). In both cases, the actual act of writing, as well as its product, were so absent from my public existence—the only realm in which personalities were noted and codified—that they didn't factor into what one might call my "identity." Nobody—myself included—ever romantically branded my unsolicited analyses of people and events at home and the eternal daydream within which I moved at school as the rumblings of an inventive mind; they were simply signs of room for improvement.

Upon graduating from junior high school—the ninth grade—everyone traded bulk-printed cards, each of which bore an individual graduation photograph. It was the custom to write a little something on the back of the card you gave someone. Three years earlier, graduating sixth grade, we'd gone round to teachers and classmates, asking them to sign our autograph albums. But in an autograph album you were only expected to write, before signing your name, one of the jingles that everybody else wrote—something like, "Don't ever kiss by the garden gate, 'cause love is blind, but the neighbors ain't." On the back of the photograph cards, the nugget of advice at least pretended to be personal and sincere, despite its almost universal dissemination. (The most common message, for example, was: "You're a great kid—don't ever change.")

I couldn't understand why people deliberately wrote such crude messages that had nothing to do with the recipients, but I never doubted that there was a good reason. In general, I assumed that the people who surrounded me in everyday life were more perceptive than they seemed to be—and just pretended to be dumb because vacuity, delivered with gusto, was the social glue that held people

together in nodding agreement. To fit in, then, I, too, would sometimes mouth vapid pieties in a cheerfully insentient way, and these
were accepted as the passport to inclusion in common humanity.

Still, each time someone asked me to write an inscription on the
back of my photo card, I couldn't help writing something specific
that I had actually noticed about the person. The result was that
each time someone handed me a card with her photo on the front
and "You're quiet but a great kid, don't ever change" on the back
(and I felt freshly slapped with disappointment, each time, that this
was all someone had to say after all those years of going to school
with me), the card I handed *her* invariably described something I
found intriguingly quirky about her character. Though I rarely said
much, I observed my classmates with the close attention of that
other, more famous Harriet—the Spy—with whom I always felt
identified.

But unlike the other Harriet, I only noted complimentary findings
on those graduation cards and kept my copious critical reflections
locked in my head. (Harriet the Spy had her diary stolen and everyone ostracized her when they read the unflattering things she had
written about them.) So even though I had transgressed junior high
school mores with my unique greetings, I was agreeably stunned to
find that people *really read* their cards, with serious, rapt looks on
their faces. Then they looked up at me with a combination of pleasure, surprise, bewilderment, and—most striking of all—curiosity. I,
the unlikely custodian of such visions, was rewarded for the first time
with the heady experience of *being seen back*. The part of me that I
usually kept quarantined as unfit for mass consumption was, however
fleetingly, publicized. Not only that, but appreciated.

However, despite the favorable reception of my cards, there turned
out to be no resulting new friendships or stratum of social life for me.

Over the years that followed, I made the discovery that there were
in fact a number of people on the Earth who did not converse in the
whiny, obtuse cadences of Long Island. During those years, I started
to publish my writing: short stories, theatre and book reviews, feminist and left-wing journalism. (Out in the world, I had developed a
Consciousness—something of great use for any writer.) I also started
to want to be famous.

The reason I wanted to be famous was not to garner the adoration of millions (though I would not have objected to that), but to catch the attention of specific literary individuals and intellectuals I wanted to know. I felt, for instance, that I would have a lot to say to Doris Lessing if only I had the opportunity. But unless I were famous, Doris Lessing would not know that I existed, would not know what sort of conversation we could have, and thus we would not have it. Unless I were famous, I would always look at people like Doris Lessing through a one-way mirror, yearning hopelessly to be looked back at—to be mutually recognized.

The person I wanted to have a conversation with more than anyone in the world was the poet and essayist Adrienne Rich. If I had had anyone in my actual life who thought and spoke with the complexity, the seriousness, the moral intensity, the meticulous language of Rich, I would not have longed so desperately for this conversation. But I had no such person.

Unable to have the real interchange with Rich that I wanted, I internalized her. In my head, even in nighttime dreams, she approved of things about me that nobody in reality did: my need for solitude; my tendency to prioritize reading and writing over social relations; my inability to go with the flow about matters that seemed highly significant to me, even if they did to no one else; my inability to distinguish between describing life and living it; my moral agonizing about virtually everything; my eccentric interpretations of people and events; my drive to use language precisely, not carelessly; my being a lesbian. In short: my struggle to take myself seriously.

But after I published my first few stories and articles in feminist periodicals—and after, conveniently and unbelievably, Adrienne Rich just happened to move into the house across the street from mine in a small, rural, New England village (I'm not kidding—this really happened)—she *knew* me. She initiated conversations with me in the tiny village post office. She came into my house to get an article she needed. She sat in on a course that I was sitting in on at a local college. Once, she prefaced a remark she made there with, "As Harriet was saying. . . ." Some years later, when we'd both moved away, I saw her at a benefit literary reading in New York. She was sitting with another feminist writer and asked if we knew each other. The two of us sheepishly shook our heads, and she introduced us, saying, "Anyway, I'm sure you know each other's work!"

Adrienne Rich is so generous and encouraging to other writers that it's hard to know whether she actually finds your work worthwhile or is just boosting your self-confidence. She had said nothing, in fact, to indicate she thought my work was any good, only that it was, as they say, "out there." In any event, her magnificent introduction had its effect. I felt welcomed by her into the circle of people who are mutually known because they have each injected into the world some imaginative artifact that has been sopped up by others. In that magic circle, irrespective of my usual human failings, I glowingly felt that I existed.

It is against the backdrop of this lifelong quest to be *seen* and *talked back to* as a writer, by the writers I most obsessively *saw* and *needed to know*, that I now introduce the adventure that took me all the way through the looking glass.

In 1989, by pure chance, I came across a small, intriguing volume in the fiction section of my local independent bookstore and impulsively bought it. Published in Australia in 1975, it was a now out-of-print lesbian coming-of-age novel called *All That False Instruction*, written by Elizabeth Riley, a writer I had never heard of. While the narrative had a strong autobiographical flavor, there was no author's bio. The novel was smart, funny, heartbreaking, and disarmingly literate; I fell completely in love with it. Years later, this is how I described my initial encounter with *ATFI* in an article for the *Women's Review of Books*:

> Reading, I'm immediately charmed by a particular fusion of humor and pathos I haven't encountered in other lesbian novels I've read. Riley's narrator-protagonist Maureen Craig couches her confessions in wry self-deprecation, exposing herself as a Woody Allenish, Charlie Chaplinesque schlemiel whose intelligence and hypersensitivity saturate her with an excruciating consciousness of her failed attempts to garner love. . . . [T]he narrative traces her development through, and just beyond, her college years in stiflingly conformist mid-1960s Australia.

> All That False Instruction is, in many ways, an archetypal out-
> sider's *bildungsroman*, in which feeling and desire, transgressive
> and suppressed, are ultimately resurrected as moral imperatives
> of their own. (WRB, 34)

For years and years, I tried to find out—from any Australian fem-
inists, lesbians, and literary folks I met—who this Elizabeth Riley was.
Many knew of the novel and that its author had produced nothing
else. But that was all. Then, in early 2000, promotional emails from a
feminist publisher in Melbourne began appearing in my inbox; it
occurred to me to hit "reply" and pose my old question. This time I
got an answer. Elizabeth Riley was a pseudonym, the publisher told
me; the author was really Kerryn Higgs, now living in New South
Wales. This publisher had in fact approached her several times about
bringing the book back into print, but some logistical problem had
stood in the way. She offered to pass on a letter from me if I wished
to send one.

After hastily securing a green light from my editor at *The Women's
Review of Books*, I wrote to Kerryn telling her (a) how much I had
loved her book for eleven years, and (b) that I would like to write an
article on the book, what had become of it, and what had become of
her. "Only if there's a good story there," had been my editor's caveat
when tentatively agreeing to run something about a long out-of-print
book that nobody in the United States had ever heard of.

There *was* a good story; as an email correspondence instantly
sprang up between Kerryn and myself, I began to piece it together.
The book had been awarded a major literary prize in its development
stage in the early 1970s. Media and family members had trumpeted
the news of the incipient novel before becoming apprised of its lesbian content. When the novel's subject matter was revealed and
Kerryn's mother threatened a libel suit, Kerryn and her publishers
heeded legal advice to release the book under a pseudonym and
moved the narrative's locale from Melbourne to Sydney. Kerryn
retreated to the shelter of anonymity with (as she confessed in one
email to me) some relief while her publishers grimly tried to market
a novel severed from both its prizewinning glory and a live author to
promote it. Capitalizing on its notoriety as Australia's first overtly

lesbian novel, they inserted the subtitle "A Novel of Lesbian Love" in lurid hot pink lettering on the dust jacket—a move that did not make the author happy.

As I swiftly gathered that Kerryn was not one to toot her own horn, I used what I now knew and newly available research methods to uncover the more illustrious facets of the book's history. "I have always been disappointed that *ATFI* sank like a stone," she wrote in her first email, leading me to believe that no one beside myself had recognized its importance. But in fact, despite the overwhelming set-backs the novel faced coming into the world, it had become an under-ground lesbian classic. It eventually appeared in paperback and in a German edition and drew much critical interest in both the popular and intellectual press of Australia and Great Britain. Its frank language and sexuality offended the occasional male critic—"That the lady can write well is abundantly apparent," one grudgingly wrote, but added that "a deliberate predilection for gutter language" made it "repug-nant." But most who wrote about it found those same qualities—along with the book's many other attributes—to be breathtakingly welcome. It probably would have achieved wider recognition had it been reissued in 1989, when the publisher wanted to include it in a new paperback series of Australian fiction, but Kerryn once again balked at the use of her real name while her parents were still alive, and the plan was abandoned.

I was amazed and very deeply moved that I was not only getting the information about *ATFI* and its author that I'd sought for so long but getting it straight from the horse's mouth. No matter how much she told me about the book and about herself, I always asked for more. This was partly because I was ragingly curious, and partly because I didn't want our business to be finished and the correspon-dence to end. I am not the kind of person who ever says things like, "I don't want to pry," because I like to pry. So I bombarded her with questions, and they went further and further afield of what I needed to know for my article.

In between bombardments, I had the good grace to apologize for taking up so much of her time and energy. But as it turned out, the timing was right. She was just beginning to emerge from a six-month depression triggered by her father's death and seized upon our correspondence as a way to further pull out of it. "I have been in a miserable state really since dad died, apathetic and very unlike myself—or what I have always taken for myself," she wrote. "You happen to catch me at a loose end where cryptic crosswords and cricket matches have been the most entertaining part of many days." I instantly wrote back asking her who she "took herself" to be, and she obligingly supplied a description. "Feels like I'm having a conversation with you that goes well beyond your project—there being no clear demarcation!" she wrote in an email she titled "no clear demarcation." But she sounded pleased and also asked me about myself. ("Must say, one little question CAN set you off on a Tolstoyan response!" she remarked when confronted with my prolific replies.) I wrote: "I'm 45, a little bit of a New York Jewish stereotype (neurotic, high-strung, talk fast and a lot, gesture a lot—I don't know if you HAVE such a stereotype out there in the Australian bush), left and feminist politics—these days, most riveted on the 'left' part."

After a few references intended, it seemed, to assure me that some of her best friends were Jewish, she wrote back:

> Your world and concerns feel very accessible and even similar to mine: eg globalisation/corporatisation you speak of re Unis, in full swing here too with the decline of humanities in the vocational/economic-rationalist trend (despite our more socialist heritage in Aus—fast decaying however). We both belong to a left-feminist culture perhaps, common across western countries, a more benign aspect of globalisation.

But politics were only one of our serendipitous commonalities. We wrote—every day, I might add—about writing, language, parental loss, Jane Campion films, Prozac, class, reconciliation, rain forest ecology, Australian shiraz. I have to admit that it took me a number of emails before I casually mentioned, as if it were a peripheral detail, that I lived with someone in a relationship of fourteen years' duration. In truth, the relationship was in its death throes, and I let it be known that there was trouble in paradise. She, for her part, mentioned casually that she was a long-term loner and a smoker.

The Kerryn that emerged through her emails struck me as very different from Maureen Craig, her fictional alter ego in *ATFI*. She sounded, in fact, bafflingly serene and well-adjusted. She now used a great many exclamation points in her writing, which gave the impression of lightheartedness, and a kind of shorthand—part Aussie slang (as in "uni" for "university"), part like someone who didn't want to be bothered with needless articles and pronouns when a point could be gotten across just as well without them—that gave her an air of cheerful briskness. (Later on, she would tell me that she had labored hard at editing each of these emails before sending them.) At one point she even commented to me that she was in fact rather ordinary, and that Maureen Craig had simply been a portrait of herself as a youngster, thirty years in the past. *Ordinary?* I responded, with a disappointment I didn't bother to conceal, desperately wanting her to take it back. "Sorry, really sorry to be crushing re ordinariness," she wrote back hastily. "Didn't mean anything like 'normal,' more that I feel I'm still bogged down in my bullshit, rather than transcending it as heroes must. Feel the 'ordinary' state of humans is to be bogged down." What a relief! I could still relate to her.

I had written to her, with false ingenuousness, everything that I thought was endearing about Maureen Craig—as if I were speaking of some third party. Kerryn was amazed and delighted that someone would warm to such a warts-and-all presentation—and that the partiality came not *in spite of* the traits that always got her into trouble, and which, she said, she usually tried to hide from people until she knew them better, but *because* of them. Every word I wrote was the absolute truth; yet because I knew that the character Maureen Craig greatly valued warm people, I was particularly uninhibited in exhibiting my warmth. I also knew that she was a country girl who had grown up amidst, and still loved, the great outdoors; she still seemed to camp a lot. I made it clear that I, too, venerated nature, though I couldn't get to it often enough from Brooklyn. "Hardly anybody wants to camp with me anymore—certainly not Sara," I wrote plaintively and completely misleadingly, since I had no more desire to sleep in a tent than Sara, my long-term partner, did. But I fantasized that maybe Kerryn would feel sorry for me, so bush-deprived, and invite me for a completely implausible camping trip in the outback.

We went on like this for about five weeks, our allusions to a deeper intimacy we both increasingly felt couched in ostensibly ambiguous but actually quite puerile terms and email subject lines, language that said things in such a way that we could claim we hadn't said them. "Happy Anniversary" was how I titled my email announcing that this "mad" correspondence had been taking place for precisely one month. "Unreasonably hot" was her title for an email partly about how climate change had brought uncharacteristically sizzling autumn temperatures to New South Wales. It was, however, her complete misinterpretation of an innocent use of the term "slippery slope" on my part (she didn't know that it referred to a logical fallacy) that made her feel the day of reckoning was at hand. Finally, we experienced a phenomenon we called Escalation: that is, we directly confronted our feelings for each other, feelings that we were both quite sure we had despite the fact that we'd never met, spoken, or seen pictures of each other, and lived, both in terms of north and south *and* east and west, on opposite ends of the world.

In the totally stupid but, for me at the time, absolutely engrossing movie *You've Got Mail*, Meg Ryan falls in love with a stranger on email, having no idea that he's actually Tom Hanks, a man she knows and detests. In one scene Hanks, goading her about the illusory nature of her email romance, asks her how she would feel if, upon meeting the man in person, she were to discover that he was fat. "I don't care about that," she says with total conviction, and I know exactly how she feels. "You don't care that he's so fat, he's one of these guys that has to be removed from his house by a crane?" he asks. "That is very unlikely," she replies realistically.

The uncanny thing about falling in love on email is that you have all the symptoms of love but without the usual hard data to go on. Is it *more* real—because you've genuinely peered into someone's mind and soul, regardless of what they look like and talk like? Or is it *less* real—because words on paper or a screen are incapable of capturing the fullness of human individuality? When you meet someone at a party and feel "that chemistry," it's not like you really have much more to go on. Most people do, in fact, "create" themselves in order to attract someone in person—through clothes, grooming, conversation—in a way that is simply an alternative to "creating" themselves online with words—with the help of spell-check, thesaurus, and time to ponder the wisdom of what they've written (even run it by a friend) before hitting "Send." Furthermore, most people do "fall in love" while still in the state of heightened illusion, and tend to feel, in retrospect, that they only discovered the "reality" of their lover once they were well into it. Isn't it possible that the illusion of the textual lover is only a different part of the elephant that the blind man feels, one port of entry among others to the same animal?

When you fall in love on email, if you are going to pursue the relationship, you have to ease into it gradually. I realize that most people who experience this phenomenon meet in chat rooms or online dating services, and that many of them follow protocols particular to those communities. But I think Kerryn and I must have been fairly typical in finally deciding, at the point of Escalation, that the next thing we wanted to do was to exchange pictures and have a phone conversation. Kerryn's techno-savvy sister put a few photos of her up on the family Web site. I, at a loss for better alternatives, referred Kerryn to an old Web page from an academic conference to which I'd hastily submitted a picture that had been taken in Alaska; the six layers of clothing I was wearing gave me the bulk of a polar bear. So there was our first, but relatively mild shock: *that's* what you look like! I mean, I knew intellectually that she had red hair, but there it was, red!

And then our first real-voice contact: the biggest shock yet. Don't ask me why, but it was jolting to hear that she had an Australian accent. (I read everything she wrote in an American accent though my brain had also somehow translated much of her writing into a clipped, upper-class British accent. Of course, that was ridiculous; she had, just as I should have expected, the sort of broad, working-class, rural Aussie accent that turns mundane vowels into astonishing diphthongs.) We stayed on the phone for two hours, trying hard to make our connection work, but through it all I fought a wave of sadness and loss. Who was this imposter, speaking to me so insinuatingly, as if she knew me? How had she learned all these things about me? When I said her name, it felt like I was taking it in vain, violating the exalted being to whom it really belonged.

We just didn't have the *access* to each other that we always had on email.

After we hung up, pretending that all had been fine (because of course, this Voice and I were polite strangers), I didn't know what to do or whom to talk to in my desolation. And then I thought of the one person who could make me feel better: the Kerryn that I knew on email. Because she still had to exist. If I could just crawl back onto email and pour it all out to her, it would surely be a good thing. So I did. She wrote back:

> Your thoughts rang true. I know I found your accent much softer than I expected, and like you, it wasn't the voice I've been writing to—though of course it IS. This happens, one chap I'd listened to for years on RN [Radio National], finally saw him on TV not long ago and absolutely couldn't match the person with the voice. Still can't, I have a double take and picture him as I always did. Anyway, for us, this morning was the first of anything concrete (not that the writing isn't in its own way), so could be something that time will change. It is a pretty mad way to meet. But certainly 21st century and vanguard.

We both felt better for having confided in each other the thoughts we couldn't possibly have shared with the alien on the phone and agreed that the best thing to do would be to try again. So the next day, we had another phone conversation, and this time it was much better. Phone talk became a part of our routine, along with email, so that we developed a real and vibrant speaking dynamic that soon lost its dependence on our written one, and we started to hear each other's true accents when we read each other's emails. Soon there was fluidity between phone calls and emails.

Then (to try to make a long story short), I managed to persuade the wonderful feminist provost of my university to fund me to go to Australia so that I could interview Kerryn in person. (Remember the article?) And don't imagine that I was a complete creep about my relationship with Sara; I came clean about everything, and we faced the fact that the end of our relationship had been dangling in front of us for a long time, though I had taken the usual weak, shallow, cowardly way out by hanging on by a thread until another relationship appeared, which is a tactic I generally despise in people. But that's another story.

With Kerryn, the transition from email to phone gave us—or me, anyway, who obsessed about it continually—a sense of what to expect of the transition from phone to Reality (as I had referred to it for some time in advance, trying to foresee and thoroughly analyze all the pitfalls in store as if that would diminish their devastating effects). "This isn't *my* body any more, it's my mother's," I warned her, anxious about my first tryst in a decade and a half. She let me know that she was short—"I'm a midget," she said once, and for a second I thought, "Does she mean that literally?"—and then, like Meg Ryan, I told myself, "I don't care. I don't care." (She didn't mean it literally.)

As my plane made its descent to Sydney, I looked at my pictures of her and leafed through the old copy of her book that I'd had all those years, knowing that this was the last time I'd ever perceive them the way I had. I knew it was very, very unlikely that the person I was about to meet could really be identical—not just in looks but in ineffable personhood—to the image I had inside me to which I was so attached. I knew that in just a few minutes, someone very beloved to me would cease to exist, and with a strange sort of mourning, as the plane landed, I said my good-byes. Then I went out into Reality and met her.

And yes, it was another weird transition, as such things must always be.

One thing I often fruitlessly wonder about is how it would have been if we had met each other first, somehow, in the real world. Would we have "recognized" each other as The Right One? Would there have been an attraction? Would we have become friends? Just how *would* we have perceived one another? I find it maddening that I will never know, though I have to remind myself that the way we *did* meet and "recognize" each other was as Real as anything else—as Real in its own way, as I've said, as meeting at a party. It was at least as normal as a wisely arranged marriage, in which the carefully considered premises of the match yield the heat that more profoundly solders the pair together over time. (Actually, I arrived in Sydney feeling bizarrely like a mail order bride.) Perhaps, for someone who has always escaped from Reality into written texts, it feels kind of funny to make the reverse passage from written texts into Reality. Where do you go from there?

In any case, we *did* make the transition to Reality, and as Jane Eyre might say if she were an online lesbian today: Reader, I married her.

Not only that, but the article came out, *All That False Instruction* was republished by the feminist publisher in Melbourne who had connected us, the new edition bore Kerryn's real name and an afterword in which she explained the whole story behind the first edition, the novel's plot was relocated back from Sydney to Melbourne, where it had been set in the first place, I wrote the critical introduction, the Australian media hailed the return of a "lost Australian classic," I have a life in Australia, and Kerryn has a life in New York.

Besides all that, when people ask me how we met, and I tell them the story, they usually say, "That's a great story!" And I realize how much it means to me that just as out of narrative, I got Kerryn, out of Kerryn, I got narrative. Kerryn and narrative: I love them both dearly.

Work Cited

Harriet Malinowitz. "Out in the Outback." *The Women's Review of Books* 17, nos. 10–11 (July 2000).

The Time of Lies
Janet Eldred

Janet Eldred practices all things writing at the University of Kentucky. In addition to directing the campuswide Writing Initiative and the Writing Center, she teaches courses in creative nonfiction and editing. In her spare time, she reads and writes, preferably at a place near an ocean. She's at work on a book that profiles Azoreans and Azorean-Americans, a project that allows her to experience the places, people, and food that she loves.

Part I. Chatham, Kent

Big lies take time to gather steam and grow to the point that they can't help but be found out, so I can't claim to know exactly when the fabrications started. Still, I remember the events that prompted the investigations. We have two sons, boys we adopted from a Russian orphanage. My older son, he's fifteen now, has sung for some time in an Episcopal men and boys choir. On Wednesdays his choir practiced, and the congregation sponsored its weekly family dinners. Over several weeks, a few of the choir teens had been crossing into the dinner room, eating, and returning innocently to practice. They weren't caught, until one Wednesday evening early in the fall, when my son decided to add some drama to the event.

The next morning I received an email message from the choir director, "Call me." I knew better than to even try to imagine the nature of the trouble my sons could find. Once, when my boys were younger, maybe eight and six, I had taken them to one of those MacDonald's playlands. That particular day, I was deep in a book when a man tapped me on the shoulder. He was livid. His daughter was having a birthday party, and my boys were on the top level of the jungle-gym structure, spitting down on the cake at the table below.

I was hoping the call from the choir director was a courtesy call, something along the lines of, "You forgot to pay for his tie," but I suspected I was paid up. The choirmaster began with the immediate problem: an elderly woman in the congregation had driven to church that morning to deliver a hot meal for that "poor boy, William." Then the choirmaster backfilled the story. "William"—my son no longer used any of his Russian nicknames—had told the woman his life story: He was born in Chatham, Kent, in Great Britain; his parents had both been killed, his brother electrocuted, all for political reasons. He was grateful for the church's Wednesday night dinners because he was an orphan with "few means and little access to food." To be fair, William denies he ever said that last part, although I doubt it. He is dramatic and overly influenced by film adaptations of Dickens' novels.

Now all kids lie. Parents do too. Yet the period I have come to call The Time of Lies was fundamentally different. We weren't talking the small, venial lie; we were talking whoppers, bordering on the pathological. When I found out about The Lies, of course I had to confront him.

"But did you really say that your brother was electrocuted?"

"Yes." He smiled, a smile of brotherly affection that said *It's what the little turd deserves.*

"And you said your parents were dead?"

"Yes."

"Why?" It seemed the only question worth asking, given the bizarre world he had created.

"They might as well be. I'll never see them."

Until such moments, one forgets that teens are simultaneously incredibly superficial and quite deep. They venture into philosophical and emotional ground where adults fear to tread.

I was taken aback. I paused, though not long enough for a thoughtful response. "Since we don't know, we shall take the positive side and presume them alive."

I knew that didn't settle it, but nonetheless I pressed on.

"And so you said you were British?"

"Yes."

"Why?"

"Because," he said. "I'm from a country that no longer exists."

To this, I could say nothing. In 1995, when I took him out of Russia, the red Soviet passport issued him was a fiction. The Soviet Union had already collapsed; Russia and the Commonwealth of Independent States (CIS) had been born four years earlier.

Part II. Faking It

Nothing on the international adoption Web sites or in the many adoption books prepared me for this particular scene. And I had studied, hard. The experts all agree: adoptees who know and celebrate their heritage will be self confident, well-adjusted, happy. We're good parents, or at least we try to be. We promised all sorts of people, from social workers to the orphanage director to Russian regional and district officials, that we would teach our children to celebrate their heritage, though granted we hedged some; we meant artsy Russia, Tsar Russia, democratic Russia, Disneyland Russia, not the grim Soviet Union. We meant every word of our promises. We started off well, buying children's books and music, taking beginning language lessons, establishing relationships with other Russians living in the United States. For years, I faithfully visited the Families of Russian and Ukrainian Adoptees Web site and ordered the resources they recommended. I have spread my dining table with *zakuski*, an elegant

Russian version of smorgasbord, many a New Year's Eve. I knew about culture camps. I knew that some adoption agencies were sponsoring guided homeland tours of Russia or Romania or India. I was determined to produce perfect, well-adjusted children, and at one point, all this attention to heritage seemed to me a surefire way to guarantee my children their healthy adoptive identities.

At the beginning, I did heritage activities religiously. Actually, that's not strictly true. It took me some time to reach that point. Like many white folk who have considered international adoption from Russia, my first impulse was just to keep the whole heritage thing a secret. My adopted kids look vaguely like me (*exactly* like me, some friends say), why not simply adopt them fully by erasing any previous ownership, by living that brilliant fiction that they have always been, will always be mine? It's a rookie mistake, this idea that you can own children, and it's one not just made by adoptive parents. We were schooled out of this naïveté during our home study. I'm a good student: they easily moved me from Point A (no heritage) to Point B (all heritage, all the time).

Our older son was almost three when we adopted him, the younger two and a half. I was a pretty good parent of young children, but here's my secret. As my children have moved into their teenage years, I've lapsed, fallen into sacrilege, buckled under the pressure of their emerging strong, young adult selves. Here's what really goes on inside our house. Occasionally, well actually rarely, we'll listen to a tape or flip through a book we can't read. More frequently, the books and tapes sit, collecting dust with all our other collectibles. Our language lessons, after a pretty good start, have come to a pretty good halt. Our contact with our Russian friends—just as it is with most of our friends—is haphazard and schedule-driven. I fantasize about return trips to Russia, kids in tow, which I'm pretty sure we'll never take. I confess, I might be questioning the whole heritage project because I'm not very good at it. I'm fascinated by Russian history and language and culture, but, I'm fascinated by many things as is evidenced by the number of aborted projects in my home: the vintage suit I cut out but never sewed, the dog who's half-trained, the bird who doesn't talk, the multiple book projects half written, or "in process," as I prefer to say.

Or maybe, in my defense, I have been slovenly because some-where along the line, I began to doubt the heritage project, or at least the simple catechism I had professed. I am incapable, it seems, of sus-taining faith, particularly when I feel I'm faking it, and the whole her-itage thing more often than not felt fake. No matter how many fur hats I donned, how many pieces of amber I had strung into a necklace, how many *matrioshka* charms I added to my bracelet, I felt like a Russian fraud. What is more, I had suspected for some time that other adoptive parents were making the same discovery, that I was not the only failed fraud. Why else would the Russian district official during our second adoption make me repeatedly confirm that I would duti-fully send postplacement reports. "Not just stories," he emphasized, "facts. Like facts from doctors. Teachers. . . ."

"Yes, of course, we will," I assured him. I certainly had sent all the required postplacements for our first adoption while preparing for the second. He knew this. Was he questioning my reporting skills? The official was stern and made me repeat the assurance several times. Then he made me sign a sheet of paper indicating that I would send in reports after three months, after six months, and yearly thereafter until the child is six or ten or some magic number I no longer remem-ber. The adoption facilitator who doubled as our translator under-scored the importance of the task: "We must have this information," he told me. "People get busy and forget. It makes it difficult for other parents wanting to adopt. We have to know these children are being cared for." It's an absolutely reasonable request. If we sent U.S. chil-dren to live with our former enemies turned ostensible allies, wouldn't we want to be assured that they were flourishing?

For some time, I was pretty methodical about postplacement reports, but after a time, I started relegating the requests to the things-to-do pile. Some years ago, frustrated after not hearing from us for two years, the agency called about our delinquent postplacement reports. My husband answered all the social worker's phone ques-tions, and I sent them photos. I collected the data from the doctor's office and the school, but I am not sure that I ever got as far as send-ing them. Surely, those schooled in modern psychology would argue that this resistance stems from something different—perhaps from deep-seated anxiety about our sons' origins? Well, yes, of course; that doesn't take a Ph.D. Yes, there is some bone in my adoptive mother body that hums, "Aren't they, after all this time, aren't they *ours*, completely ours?" I admit that it requires a conscious effort to stave off this feeling. I try hard to remind myself that there are birth mothers, I try to imagine their lives. At points in my mothering life, I have thought so much about my children's mothers that I can hear them speak to me. I'm well aware of the dear, the precious, the expensive nature of their loss, my gift. It's an unforgettable tragedy. Yet during bad stretches, times when life ticks on in predictable ways, my keen sense of my children's origins becomes some kind of primordial human appendage I carry with me but no longer use. We're an ordinary family, living an ordinary bourgeois life; why this compulsion to report? What can be said that is remotely interesting? Why the necessity of finding others with credentials to speak for me? I am capable of speaking, if there's something to be said, but sometimes, even I am bored by the ordinariness of our lives. I prefer it that way.

Still finally, I thought, this wasn't about me—it was about my kids: I was doing all this for them, and they were authentic Russians, the real articles, or so I believed.

Part III. Newton's Third Law, Revised, "For Every Story, There Is an Equal and Opposite Story"

Truth, I find, is held in equilibrium by stories. Heritage projects aren't action plans, they're reaction plans, or ideally proactive cures to a potentially rampant social disease. Bad press haunts orphan children. In the case of children from the Eastern bloc countries, the specifics go something like this: The Communists dumped children in sterile, institutional settings, where they languished—granted, fed, clothed, and medicated—but otherwise ignored. The Romanian dictator had the most developed and devious plan. He was rumored to be purposefully raising antisocial orphans to fill the ranks of his secret police.

As Americans, we fall easily into villainous tales about communism. Yet this wasn't what I witnessed when I saw the orphanage where my sons were raised for almost three years of their childhood— there was a music room, for instance, and any number of babushkas running behind the children, wiping noses, and so on. Nonetheless, it's the horror stories that have survived, forming an unstated backdrop to my children's personal histories. *Oh, an orphanage in Russia. Oh*—concerned pause—*are they okay?* Behind *that* innocent question is the assumption that all adopted kids have problems; Eastern bloc kids just have a specific malady.

If an adoptive country is telling international orphans that they are more likely to be "disturbed" than biological children—and ours is with some frequency—might this not produce disturbed children? I find myself irritated, then moved to anger, when I read something like the *New York* magazine article about adoptees from Eastern Europe. The cover featured an out-of-focus picture of a child, running toward the camera, its facial features an indiscernible blur. The large block letters read, "Detached, Disturbed, Unreachable." Inside, the reporter recounted in sensational detail the troubling story of attachment disorder. If these were my children on the cover (were they?), what hope have we for the future?

Such a leap, you think. *Those aren't your children.*

But they are. In fact, I would argue that they are the children of anyone even pondering adoption from Eastern Europe. Consider an email I received from a former student.

Hi Dr. Eldred,

I was in an English class that you taught about 7 or so years ago. I remembered that you and your husband had adopted two children from Russia. My husband and I are considering Russian adoption as well. . . . How are they doing now? Was it a shock for them to come to your home?

I don't know if it's good or bad, but I have been doing a lot of internet research on adopting a 4-6 year old. There is a myriad of information regarding emotional issues that children have from growing in an institution-like environment. Specifically, there are a lot of children with severe attachment issues . . . they don't trust that you will meet their needs, etc. Some of the personal accounts are terrifying. . . . citing actions like cruelty to animals, lying, stealing, self-hate, etc. My husband and I are getting a little nervous. My husband is a psychologist, but unfortunately an experimental one . . . he gives me blank stares when I ask these questions. I understand that this is a very personal issue and I certainly respect your rights to keep your life private. However, if you have any suggestions I would greatly appreciate them.

She is clearly nervous, frightened even, and why wouldn't she be? Prospective or current adoptive parents research and read books like *Broken Spirits Lost Souls: Loving Children with Attachment and Bonding Difficulties.* The author comes with credentials. She's an "RN, MA, and counseling graduate from Rhode Island College," an authority who has some thirty years experience "loving powerful and disturbed youngsters." The book's marketing blurb tells readers that children "born into crisis" are "vulnerable to attachment disturbances." What exactly does this mean? The blurb explains. Children with reactive attachment disorder (RAD) "represent the embryonic stages of an antisocial personality: at their worst they are full-blown psychopaths all consumed by their search for yet another victim." Put this information together with other research that links RAD to orphans from Eastern bloc countries, and wham! instant fear, suspicion. The author warns us that RAD is "not nearly as rare as we pray." Just look around. Notice those "out-of-control three-year olds"—the kind who might spit on a little girl's birthday cake—and follow their real-world drama as they become teens who "defy authority and challenge every accepted familial and societal norm." *I'm British. Born in Chatham, Kent.*

"But you're just raising a gifted kid," my friends reassure me. "He's imaginative." I like this idea. Yet in my darker moments, I wonder, Am I raising a talented kid? Or the talented Mr. Ripley?

As with most of these books, *Broken Spirits Lost Souls* promises a method of prevention: "simple, sound parenting skills." Whew! No wonder prospective parents cling to such books. But here's the rub: For parents who have adopted internationally, the "simple, sound parenting skills" rest on the foundation of heritage. Only pride in heritage, a strong sense of self—the two are equated—can make up for the lack of affection these children are presumed to have experienced in sterile, institutional orphanages. The celebratory culture camps create for "foreign" adoptees idealized origins whence magically spring organic strong identities. Just how parents are supposed to explain how this wonderful homeland allowed them to languish, unloved, is never confronted. Instead, explanations tend to assume dream logic. The solid connections dissolve in daylight. But I'm being too hard here. Culture camp and other heritage programs offer hope in place of fear and suspicion, and hope is a better foundation for family.

So here I sit, immobilized between two stories. I can't bring myself to embrace the small-world culture camps, and yet I can't laugh away the fact that I have failed the heritage thing.

Part IV. Disequilibrium,
or, The Impossibility of Getting the Story Right

Almost immediately after adopting our first child, I wrote about the experience and after a time published my reflections in a book alongside essays about the other oddities in my life, my mother, my father, neighbors, and so on. I edited that book with an awareness that my children would someday read it. In 2005 when it was published, some day seemed far off. I felt that both my sons were still too young to read it (my younger son was just eleven), but bits of it leaked out to them just the same. A year later the book was entirely outed when my older son asked me for a copy to give to his English teacher. This request came during The Time of Lies, William's freshman year in high school. He hated his public school. He also believed he hated his father. I took comfort where I could get it: he only half-hated me. Overall, he was a case study in teen hate and misery. I took hope in the thought that he wanted to make nice with his English teacher. I gave him a copy of the book with the shrink-wrap still on it.

A few weeks later, William asked me a question, and it was clear that he had read my book.

"You never gave that book to your teacher," I scolded.

"No. I wanted to read it."

"So when, when have you been reading it?"

He read it at break, he told me, and sometimes snuck it out during class time when he was bored.

There was no pretending he hadn't read it, so I asked the question that had been lingering in the back of my mind, "What did you think?" I thought he might find it strange to run up against his life on paper. I half expected him to scold me.

"Um, it's good?"

I couldn't believe he thought I was fishing for a compliment. "No," I said. "Not that. Did I get it right? Did I tell your story right?"

"I guess," he said. "It's not like *I* remember any of it."

I said something stupid, something like "Parents are the keepers of their children's memories." I told him one day he would set his own story down.

"Uh-huh."

There are no secrets between brothers. Adoptive brothers are no different, so I knew my younger son would read the book soon. He was more articulate about his reaction, honing in on one three-letter word in the whole book. "Why did you call me *fat*?"

I hadn't realized that the word *fat*, when applied to a two-and-a-half-year-old child, could convey such a social stigma, could inspire so much angst. I had worried about important, sensitive subjects, like birth parents, for instance. "But I was just trying to describe how malnourished you were, how ironic it was that you were starving and yet you looked . . ." I almost said the *f* word, but I checked myself, then grew impatient, something I'm inclined to. "You had rickets, for God's sake. You were quite bent up. Your brother went around telling everyone he had a brother with cricket legs. You never minded *that*."

I do not need to tell you that this explanation accomplished nothing. I eventually apologized and promised to do better, adding guiltily a whispered "next time."

To my surprise, he didn't object to the idea of a "next time." "Will you put *my* picture on the cover?" he asked.

They know that I hate, loathe, and detest sibling rivalry. "Of course," I said offhandedly. I had chosen the picture of my older son for the cover because it had been taken by James Baker Hall, a Kentucky Poet Laureate and an accomplished photographer and filmmaker. Somewhere along the line, the photo had become about my son, but at the time I chose it, it was an artistic decision.

"Which picture?" my younger son asked, trying to pin me into a more specific promise, editing me even before I had written the book. Now he was pushing on my last nerve, and he knew it. I'm Azorean-American by heritage; I have a fiery Portuguese temperament. My boys love to bull bait me. They do it effectively. At such times, I'm apt to sink to the lowest parental level.

I descended, grabbing a line out of the parents' cliché bag, "The picture of you naked in the tub," I hissed.

He's a professional. It was too easy a return. He didn't hesitate, not for a nanosecond. "Won't work. My brother is in that one too."

These weren't conversations we should be having. But have them we do, with some frequency.

Part V. Everyday Rebellions

When my children started laying out editorial parameters for me, I resisted the urge to write about them, almost. I did write one short essay that featured both, but I tucked it into an academic article and published it in an anthology that only a small subset of college writing teachers will read—it would take some real sleuthing skills to ferret that one out—so that one really doesn't count. In general, I exercised restraint, until The Time of Lies.

The Time of Lies tried us all. There seemed no end to it. A month after the choir episode, I checked my son's MySpace account, and there it was again: Birthplace, Chatham, Kent. And a week later, when I had a conference with his English teacher, my American accent surprised her. It was then that I learned that William had told everyone in his class that he was born in Great Britain—Chatham, Kent naturally. At the naval base.

"Take that off your MySpace," I said. "You can't just invent a nationality."

"I'm going to get a British passport."

"You can't just *get* a passport. You need papers."

"Fine. I'll get the papers."

"You can't. You're not British. You're American. And when people ask you where you were born, you've got to tell them."

"I'll tell them I'm from Europe," he said, in a tone of voice that drew the proverbial line. This was his compromise, as low as he would go. Bottom line. Final answer. Europe.

"Eastern Europe."

"Europe."

"Why? Why can't you say that you were born in Russia?"

"Because they're losers. They lost."

William is a good student, some of the time in some subjects, but in history, his grades are always high, and his knowledge of the subject is more impressive than the grade indicates. He learned about the Cold War from U.S. sources. Corrupt communism collapsed. Democracy triumphed. We won. They lost. Everything else is just detail.

As my children grew older and spent more time with other people at school, I'm wondering how it was that I hadn't anticipated that my simple version of Heritage 101 would fail. As parents, we assume we can forge our children's identity in the world, even as we suspect the more complex truth: children form identity in a world that gives them language and impresses values on them. Parents are just one of those pressing concerns, a weighty one to be sure, yet not as hefty as social voices and national history.

It's not that there aren't cultural scripts for adoption. Ideally, adoption stories take the shape of a good romance. The adoptee feels the severance, the resulting lack, and then, falls into the arms of family. Or, in an alternate ending, the adoptee is reunited with birth parents after a long search and feels whole and alive in the world. I believe both these narratives happen, just as I believe people fall in love. I also believe William is acutely aware of "adoptive-normal" stories, particularly as he falls into plot. He's at that stage of the story in which he's less than whole; he's severed and needs to be put back together, somehow. And here's the script he's been handed: He should return to his homeland, go in search for his origins, his past, just as he should, in heteronormative standards, seek a specific future, that is, find a girl, get a degree, and settle down. But he is a teen, which means he is staging a number of small rebellions, and antiheritage is one of them. Like all good rebellions, his makes me think: What happens when a heritage romance goes awry, when the genuine feeling just isn't there? Must he, must we, fake it?

Part VI. "Knock Yourself Out"

Maybe our problem is this, that we're barking up the wrong tree. Maybe, it's not the orphans we need to reform, but the culture at large. Maybe, adoption is a better foundation for family than birth. Yet this is an increasingly difficult case to make, an increasingly difficult goal as we continue to consume, with insatiable appetite, stories of adoptions gone awry, nightmarish stories of institutes set up to protect unsuspecting parents, victims, vulnerable people who have been sucked into adopting international orphans, who presumably are incapable of love or learning or anything resembling normal childhood development. These words take shape, assume solidity. They form the cultural ground on which my family plays, and acknowledging such, I can begin to understand why British heritage sounds so attractive to my son.

My oldest son is, granted, a case of one. And yet, this case of one fascinates me because, given the numbers of international adoptees, there are bound to be more children living this internal geography.

At some point during The Time of Lies, as I worked through these musings, I came to suspect that maybe change needs to start first at home, with me. Last summer, prompted by a trip to the family cemetery in New Bedford, Massachusetts, I began planning a trip to the Azores. I'm half Azorean-American. Or maybe a quarter, since my mother's father was—scandal—French Canadian. Heritage is fluid, especially in the United States. How far back does one draw the authentic line? At what point do we become frauds, or half people searching romantically for fragments of our various missing homelands, the imagined ones that will form us into a romantic whole? How many pieces must I put together? These are big and troubling questions, but admitting I have them, even at my advanced middle age, is a start. My children, in such musings, are not that much stranger than I; they are different, as we all are, in the details.

I am tempted to say my new, more complex heritage plan, one that includes looking inward at me as well as outward at "them," has worked. At the very least, my sons seem relieved that the attention has shifted from my sporadically intense promotion of all things

Russian. While I can't claim any scientific connection to the Portuguese project—things might just have unfolded this way—I'm happy to report that we seem to have (mostly) moved beyond The Time of Lies. It happened slowly, with concessions on all sides. My older son, still miserable at his school, begged us to send him to Catholic school, the very education I begged my parents to free me from. We did. He's happy now, all uniformed up and affiliated with dramatic productions, men's choir, student government. On one of our morning drives cross town to get to the Catholic high school, I broached the issue growing in importance to me. In my head, I was composing another essay about him and his brother, this essay, but I felt the familiar guilt about writing it, about poaching on their life stories once again.

"So," I said. "My last book. How did it feel to have me writing about you?"

"Fine, I guess."

"But you were little then. Just a kid. Certainly now, now that you're older, wouldn't you mind?"

"Not really."

"Really? I can even tell the Great Britain stuff?"

"Knock yourself out." He looked perplexed that anyone would want to write anything voluntarily. Writing was something he had to do for school.

"But it's *your* story. You might want to write it."

"Yeah, whatever."

He was bored. He's living in the present, dreaming his future. Right now, he has no time for the past, no desire to have it define his present or dictate his future. He's tired of the scripts assigned to him.

I took that "yeah" as a kind of permission and wrote. Just about when I had finished the first draft, I received an email message saying that the orphanage in Russia was celebrating its twentieth anniversary, that the director and chief doctor would be celebrating their twenty-fifth wedding anniversary and their fiftieth birthdays, all within the same month. It was an appeal for money but tucked in the appeal was a plea. The group sponsoring the fund drive had interviewed the couple whose life work had been at the orphanage. The interviewers had posed the typical questions: What's the most rewarding part of your job? The hardest? The hardest came quickly to the doctor and her husband, "Not knowing what has happened to the children." Of course. Few of us can imagine how it must feel to send toddlers away in the arms of strangers, and at that, strangers who were enemies not so long in the distant past. The fund-raisers hatched a plan to organize a photo album for the occasion, with pictures of the grown orphan children matched with the photos of them as toddlers in Russia.

We received the request after the deadline for submissions (I could write another entire essay about adoption and its strange time frames), but I felt that late or not, this was a report we should write. I huddled the boys in the hallway the next morning. I explained the anniversaries and the birthdays. I told them what the director and doctor had said in response to the question about the most difficult part of their jobs. I asked them if they wanted to supply the photographs and added another task: I asked them to write to the director and the doctor themselves.

"In Russian?" my younger son asked, bewildered. He knows three words of Russian, "please," "thank you," and "good night."

"No," I replied. "In English. We'll get it translated."

There was great relief on both their parts, and then they agreed to the task quickly and enthusiastically. They seem unfazed when I suggested that we had only five days to get it done. We proceeded as if we would complete the task this time even though we all knew our track record for such things was poor. The boys worried aloud only about which picture they should send. I could barely get them to think of the writing part although the younger did say he wanted to start back on Russian lessons.

Later, in the car on the drive to school, with curiosity getting the better of me, I asked my older son what he planned to write in his letter.

"Oh," he said. "I'm going to list my activities: 'I have been in a number of dramatic productions, either acting or as assistant technical director. I have been a member of two choirs. As a treble, I received my senior ribbon in the Royal School of Church Music. I am now a tenor in the men's choir and the only tenor who sings the National Anthem for school events.' "

I suggested we might want to leave out the part about the national anthem. The orphanage director and doctor know that the children are U.S. citizens, but knowing this in theory is one thing, being presented with the details another. "Yeah," he agreed. We both wanted the director and the doctor to be reassured. My son's letter, I think, should do just that. After all, he will supply them with facts, pared down, edited, and who's to say his way isn't better? Then again, maybe, between our stories, his and mine, we hold truth in check.

"Just Like in Benheim"
Mimi Schwartz

Photo credit Stuart Schwartz

Mimi Schwartz's most recent book is Good Neighbors, Bad Times—
Echoes of My Father's German Village, *which informed this essay. Other
books include* Thoughts from a Queen-Sized Bed *and* Writing True:
The Art and Craft of Creative Nonfiction *(with Sondra Perl). Her work
has appeared in* The New York Times, The Missouri Review, Creative
Nonfiction, Fourth Genre, *and* The Writer's Chronicle, *among others.
She is a winner of the ForeWord Magazine Book of the Year Award in
Memoir 2008 and six of her essays have been Notables in Best
American Essays. A Professor Emerita of Richard Stockton College of
New Jersey, Schwartz lives in Princeton, New Jersey.*

Do you know how we did the wash? My mother had a big ket-
tle. We took it into the yard, put water in it, made the fire—and
then the wash got cooked. It took two days, the laundry, so we
didn't change our clothes so often.

Sophie Marx,[1] who grew up five houses from my father, is reminiscing about life in their little German village. "Not even toilet paper we
had!" But more than the primitive conditions, she remembers "the
wonderful mountains and forests . . . and wild flowers dancing in the
meadow" outside her window. And most important: the intimacy of
community: "Each knew each. The whole village, the Gentiles too.
They were nice, very nice. Then Hitler came."

Sophie now lives in a dimly lit, two-bedroom apartment "1B, first
left after the front door"—three blocks south of the George
Washington Bridge and five thousand miles from Benheim. Her graf-
fiti-covered, stone apartment building is in the heart of Washington
Heights, New York, where German-speaking Jews, fleeing Hitler, settled during the 1930s. The German Jews who wanted to forget
German forever, like my family—"We will speak only English!" my
father had said—headed for Queens ten miles away.

Which was fine with me. I was born in 1940, three years after they
came to America, and I found it bad enough that my parents said
"moder" and "fader" and could never master the *th* of my friends' parents. But at least they stuck to English, not like those who arrived,
sometimes one hundred strong, at my Aunt Thea's house every spring
for an annual Sunday *Nachmittag* of cake and nostalgia. I cringed. They
dressed German, spoke only German, and their smiles were too eager
as they pinched my cheek. "Little Mimi-le!" I backed away from their
foreignness but also from the chasm of grief I sensed behind their
strained optimism: for the homes they lost, the country that betrayed
them, the friends and family who didn't make it and were murdered.

I backed away from my father's memories as well, even his good
ones. Whenever he or his brothers began reminiscing, "In Benheim
before Hitler we all got along. . . ." I tuned out. His world was not

---

[1] I've changed the names of people and of the village to protect their
privacy, but all else is true.

mine, I'd mutter; and only now, half a century later, have I changed
my mind. Like it or not, I need his old world with its secrets of good
and bad to tell me who I am, could have been, and could still be.
If my father were alive, I would listen to his boyhood stories now, but
he died years ago. So I am here to ask Sophie (and whoever else I can
find) to tell me their memories.

I am late. In 1939 when Sophie came to America, there were at
least fifty Benheim Jews within twenty city blocks, offering each other
solace and information about where to find a doctor, a job, a post
office, an English class. Most have died or moved, and Sophie is the
last German Jew in her building, surrounded by neighbors from
Puerto Rico and Mexico. "They are very nice," says Sophie, now
eighty-six and still running her household, "especially since Hella
died. You remember Hella? Hella Loewengart? Your father's second
cousin, a born Tannhauser?" I look blank. "No? She lived in 3B."

Like everyone from Benheim, Sophie is playing the genealogy
game, assuming that as *die Tochter* (daughter) *von Artur Loewengart*, I
have mastered the lineage of all the 350 Jews who once lived in
Benheim. The upside is that Sophie, who I met last week at this year's
Benheim gathering (now down to twenty old people), welcomes me
like a favorite daughter. She was the first to volunteer to talk to me
about life before, during, and after Nazi times.

I am struck by how upbeat Sophie is. If I saw her outside on the
cement sidewalks dotted with garbage cans and stray litter—an old,
thin, hunched woman in a baggy dress, taking painfully small steps
from a once-broken pelvis, eyes to the ground—I would think how
miserable she must be. And yet she seems "full of beans," as my
mother would say. Sophie is the first really old person I've talked to in
years. I'm usually whizzing by as they move in slow motion, far
behind me. But lately—maybe it's my age—I'm looking over my
shoulder more often.

We are sitting next to a window that overlooks a phone booth and
the block's one, spindly tree. The window is still her favorite spot, she
says, "just like in Benheim." Always sick with asthma as a child, "and
then on the lung" (probably TB), Sophie spent many hours gazing,
while her friends were in school or in the meadows she could only
look at. "I learned to make do with less," she says without bitterness.

"Do you think my car is safe there?" I ask. My eyes are on two teenagers in backward caps, rolling joints on my parked Honda. It's the only one on this street of rusted sedans without The Club locked onto the steering wheel.

"*Ach*, safe is no place." She waves, and a hefty boy waves back. "*Aber Pablo ist ein guter Bub. Sehr gut.*" She realizes she's switched languages and apologizes. "Pablo is a good boy. His family lives upstairs. Spanish people, wonderful to me." She tells me how Pablo's father, the super, brings her the newspaper in the morning. And how another neighbor in 3E lent her a vacuum cleaner because hers has been broken for weeks. She brings him cookies. "We make do," she says, patting my hand, "just like in Benheim."

It's a big leap from little Benheim to 179th Street in Manhattan, but the connection clearly cheers her. Stuck all day in a dark room— brown sofa, brown chair, brown rug, even the window light seems swallowed up by brownness—Sophie speaks as if wild flowers still danced outside. She says again: how before Hitler everyone got along, how her neighbors were decent people, but what could they do in Nazi times? I grew up on Hollywood movies in which all Germans were murdering Nazis, so her stories, running counter to that, remind me more of my father's memories of "everyone getting along."

On top of the television sits a photo of a younger Sophie, shapely and smiling, her hair tightly permed, her head tipped toward a man with a moon face and wired glasses. "Your husband?" I ask. She nods. Fritz was born in Strasbourg and had a French passport, so that's how they got out. "The German quota was full. We would have been trapped." Fritz came first (an uncle in Ohio sent enough for one fare) and then borrowed from other Benheimers, twenty dollars here, fifty dollars there, until he could pay for Sophie's ticket. She worked weekends for years to pay back the loan, mostly in a small restaurant owned by the former butcher of Benheim where she washed dishes. "I made five dollars in two nights. Half I had to pay him, and half I could keep. We were very poor. So poor we almost gave away our baby."

She says it so softly, I almost miss it. "Give away your baby?" I ask, before I can hide my shock. What desperation she must have had! My parents had it so much easier, smuggling enough money out of Germany to get by in those start-up years. They even bought an old house when I was born—to really be American.

"*Ja*, we almost had to," she nods, embarrassed, her eyes downward. But then perks up, "But Self Help, the refugee organization, and the other Benheimers saved us!" Sophie is again all smiles, so quick is her shift from dark to light: "They paid for a tiny studio with central heat, a gas stove, an electric refrigerator —all miracles after Benheim! We had no kitchen cabinets but we made do. Everything—vinegar, salt, onions, plates and cups, everything—all fit into the big steamer trunk we brought from Germany."

Sophie gets up slowly and disappears behind a screen that, judging from the dish clatter, must be the kitchen. I watch Pablo clowning with girls on the stoop across the street until Sophie returns with a small plate of cookies. "Strictly kosher!" she assures me proudly, saying she walked ten blocks to 170th Street to get them. Given her difficulty walking, it must have been an all-day expedition. I feel honored. Although I'm not kosher, never was. My family gave that up long before they gave up German. As did everyone we knew in Queens.

Sophie watches me until I take a pink cookie. "It is good, yes?" I think of my Benheim aunts—Aunt Kaethe, Aunt Thea, Aunt Martel, all dead now—hovering over me as I tasted their specialties, the world depending on my smile of pleasure. "Delicious!" I say and take another, this time a turquoise with chocolate sprinkles that scatter on me as I beam.

So far I've shied away from the Hitler years, worried about stirring up sadness I can't control. But I want to know more about her Christian neighbors, whose families lived side by side for almost four hundred years. I want to know how much of the good memories is nostalgia, how much is real.

"Did you have any good Christian friends, growing up?" I ask, easing in.

"Not so many. But one, a nice girl, Inge."

"Did you play together much?"

"Not so much."

I try a "Tell me about" question that my sociologist friends say will draw people out. "Tell me about her family."

"Her mother was a nice woman. She gave me Christmas tree cookies once—and my mother never found out. What trouble I would have had!" She shakes her head and smiles, pointing to her cookie platter.

I take another. "But why?"

"Not kosher, of course! It was a terrible thing. I worried about it for months, waiting for God's punishment."

The power of kosher. No eating off plates that mix milk and meat, therefore no eating from "Christian" plates. Chatting in the streets, yes. Helping each other's families, yes. But no shared dining—except for the men drinking beer together at the *Gasthaus Kaiser*, owned by Jews. Kosher, I am thinking, is what helped everyone coexist in peace for centuries with no lines blurred, nothing that could turn neighbors into relatives. Falling in love, intermarriage, they were the dread of both groups. Later, in other interviews, I will learn how the Jews said the Mourner's Kaddish, the prayer for the dead, for those who crossed that line from neighborliness to something else. And how the Catholics excommunicated a young boy who loved a Jewish girl and sent another to a monastery in America. And how a Jewish girl, my father's age, was kidnapped by her father and brothers and placed on a ship to America to keep her from her Catholic shepherd; but she jumped ship, returned for him, and they ran off for good. No more than one or two such stories per generation. I attribute that to kosher.

"So how did you and Inge become friends?"

"We learned sewing together in the Sister's sewing class. They were the nuns, the Sisters, we called them. Very nice. One was the nurse who often came to see me. The other one taught us sewing. A nice woman, very nice."

Sophie is clearly not a storyteller, but her story about the sewing class does affirm "everyone getting along." Benheim Jews, she adds, also belonged to the choir, dancing classes, shooting clubs, and the fire brigade. "One was even on the village council, once."

I head into Nazi times. "Did you and Inge remain friends after Hitler came to power?" I'd love an affirming yes to prove that friendship can override politics, even in terrible times.

"Not so much."

"But you still saw each other, right?"

"Not so much." She leans away, as if to get some air. Is she hiding the bad stories? Of Kristallnacht, when the synagogues in Germany were destroyed? Of the ten Benheim Jewish men taken to Dachau concentration camp the next day? That was 1938, so Sophie was still in Benheim, but she did leave for America before the mass deportations of Jews began in 1940. "*Ich kann mich nicht mehr. . . . Entschuldigung.* I can't do more, I'm sorry" and goes on to say: "I'm an old woman, not so smart. And my English, not so good."

She stands up, and I feel like a D.A. grilling an uncooperative witness. The same thing happened when I tried interviewing my mother—she kept changing topics—and my cousin Anna, who kept saying, "I was only ten when we left Benheim. I don't remember a thing." Yet Anna spent an hour remembering everything about our clan gatherings in Baldwin, Long Island, where her father had a boat. He would take us fishing, like it or not. Which made me remember years of seasickness, except when he let me tickle the belly of a blowfish until it collapsed like a pricked balloon. Sophie's memories must, like mine, be there inside her if only I could release them.

I change my tack—"Your English is very good!"—hoping praise will give her confidence. "Did you learn it here?"

"*Ja, naturlich.* In Benheim there was no English. Only if you went to Dorn to the high school. Your father, he went. No, maybe they only learned French. *Ach,* I don't remember."

Sophie's shoulders hunch with exhaustion. *She's an old woman. Let it go!* I tell myself. But I can't. I want a story, a yes or no on the neighbors of Benheim. "It must have been hard to learn English here."

"It was. It was." She brightens at my sympathy. "I have now a home aide who comes two hours—she's Russian—and I see how hard it is for her. She speaks very little English yet, so I remember the same with me."

She moves toward a dark cabinet with a shoebox on top, ready for me. Out comes a photo of her son in Staten Island, the stockbroker, the one who went to college. Out comes her house in Benheim, an old stone house with wooden trim and chickens in front, like my Dad' s house. Nothing new here—except that Sophie is now in charge of this interview. I look at my watch.

"Here is my daughter Elsa." The photo shows a stern middle-aged woman with a cane. "And here is my grandson Richie," she says, beaming. Out comes a teenager with the same moon face as his grandfather, his arm around a smiling, dark-eyed beauty, hair piled in a thousand ringlets on her head. "They were married last year and live now in Mexico, in her village, but next month they are coming—with the baby. My fifth great-grandchild," she says with pride, holding the fingers of one hand. "A Mexican!" I listen for irony. Or anger. None. The bigotry I'd expect from a tradition-bound Benheimer isn't there, overridden perhaps by love of family, or necessity—or just by "nice" neighbors who lend a vacuum cleaner and bring a daily newspaper.

So that is the story, the one that slipped in through the side window of my expectations. I'm not yet used to that: how my great questions flop, and then while I'm putting on my coat or biting a cookie, a gem is revealed. Not the one I wished for about two little girls defying Hitler for the sake of friendship, but an odd American echo of that possibility. For despite societal barriers, an Orthodox German Jew who walks hours to buy kosher cookies has bonded with her Hispanic neighbors. And more amazing, she ignores powerful religious taboos against intermarriage to be proud of her Mexican, Catholic great grandson, Miguel.

Grandson Richie, it seems, came to live with Sophie after her other daughter's divorce (another taboo in Benheim). He fell in love with Pablo's cousin when she came to visit from Chirrapas and now the two live, with little Miguel, in her tiny mountain village, "miles from anywhere," according to Sophie's daughter who went to visit and came back distraught.

" 'Never again!' my daughter Elsa told me. 'It was so primitive, no electricity, no toilets!' " Sophie is animated in imitation. "But I told Elsa not to get so excited. It's just like in Benheim!"

There is no sign of joking. This is how life makes sense to Sophie. It's how she "made do" for eighty-six years on two continents. And how, with her big smile, the one that once scared me, she keeps fitting the incongruous pieces of Benheim, 179th Street, and Mexico together, as she passes me more pink and turquoise cookies. "So what is so bad?"

The City in the Back of the Mind

Mike Rose

Mike Rose is on the faculty of the UCLA Graduate School of Education and Information Studies. He is the recipient of a Guggenheim Fellowship and is the author of Possible Lives: The Promise of Public Education in America, The Mind at Work: Valuing the Intelligence of the American Worker, An Open Language: Selected Writing on Literacy, Learning, and Opportunity, *and, most recently,* Why School?: Reclaiming Education for All of Us. *"The City in the Back of the Mind" is part of a work in progress on imagination and memory.*

We all carry with us so many memories and stories of the past. Think of the memories. The bedroom or kitchen of your first home. Visits to grandparents or great-grandparents. Games your parents played with you. Little sayings or riddles. Something awful—a loss or injury—or something joyous. Places that had special, even magical, significance. My undergraduate assistant vividly remembers a house so eerie that, as she puts it, "it seemed to grow cold and dark on the street" as she walked by.

And there are stories—every family has them. There are the stories your parents or grandparents tell you about the old days, here or in another country. The comic stories or the tragic ones you hear around the kitchen table. There are the family stories of triumph or foible: "There was this one time when your uncle. . . ." And of course, some of these stories involve you.

What strikes me as I get older is how powerfully these memories and stories, these secrets and revelations, shape who we are and how we see the world. Sometimes we're pretty aware of this fact, and sometimes events occur that reveal to us—to our surprise—how rooted we are in memory and story. In my thirties, I began to try to get a better sense of my own past, to come to understand how its memories and stories have influenced who I am. This happened through trips back to the city where I was born: Altoona, Pennsylvania, in west-central Pennsylvania, about an hour or so east of Pittsburgh.

In one of my earliest memories of Altoona, I am sitting high up on the fire escape behind my parents' Italian restaurant looking down on the Pennsylvania Railroad shop yard, the tracks crisscrossing, the trains going in and out of the roundhouse. We couldn't have been more than two or three stories above the yard, but, in memory, the scene seems both distant and immediate, far away but with metal screeching on metal, fire shooting up through the smoke. Somewhere across town, some hazy someplace a quick car ride away, was the site of another vivid memory: my grandmother's house. I am in the garden, the first garden I had ever seen, standing among trellises and tall plants propped up with sticks. My grandmother has just killed a chicken, and its headless body is running crazily through corn stalks, Jesse, the Great Dane, barking after it.

These images stay with me, though my parents and I moved from Altoona when I was seven. They are laden with feeling. The city I carry in my mind.

I have visited Altoona many times since, for family reunions mostly, but also for a quick visit with my cousins. And as I got older, I increasingly wanted to get a better sense of the place, to fill in the fragmented map of childhood, develop scope and detail, layout and grid.

It was common on the first or second day in Altoona to take a walk through the center of town; this was where we lived, where we had our restaurant. Sometimes I walked with my mother, or a cousin, or sometimes alone. On one of those days when I wanted to clarify my sense of the city, I headed out toward the train yard, guided by a map laid out on my cousin's kitchen table the night before.

I walked down the old streets, unfamiliar in stretches. Then I'd come upon a landmark. The school where I attended first and second grade. The cathedral next to it. The ornate drugstore that marked the distant end of our block. Farther east to the diner where my father met my mother. It's still there. A loop down an alley to the back lot of our house, yellow dirt and gravel.

Our house: 1117 13th Avenue. Two stories, deep red brick. There is a back porch, which I remember, and under it a brief, dark stairway to the basement. I go down. A medical doctor used to have his office on the first floor, and I was fascinated by the things he threw away. Charts with rotating arrows, labeled boxes, rubber stoppers, syringe barrels, and, most of all, tiny pharmaceutical bottles. I kept the bottles lined up on the ledge of the basement window.

I walk back out to the alley. It is about noon by now. The building next door is a boarded-up hotel, and the sun shines bright and warm on it. The wall is cut granite for four or five feet from the ground up; then it's smooth yellow brick. I lean against it. A black fire escape sharp against the brick begins a few feet above my head. The mortar securing the granite curls out in irregular globs, like some sort of amateur pastry; a few pieces are big enough to put your fingers under. I remember this, this big, bumpy surface. I suddenly feel like someone has unshuttered a familiar room, letting bright light in.

I grew up in Los Angeles, and for a while, as a young man—long after leaving Altoona—I took up photography. Without thinking much about it, I was drawn to old places: facades and ironwork, the simple visual delight of a window set in brick, the everyday pits and cracks of an aging wall. Standing in the back lot of my old house, it strikes me how much we live in multiple landscapes, not just remember them—how our present perception is influenced by the earliest porch, field, trellis, stairway. These affect what we see and how we see it.

Like many cities in the industrial Northeast, the "rust belt," Altoona was a company town. It was developed in the mid-nineteenth century as a key link in the Pennsylvania Railroad's route from New York to Pittsburgh, the region's source of coal and iron and the gateway to the rivers of the Ohio and Mississippi valleys. From its beginnings through World War II, Altoona was, in its way, an industrial boom town. With every passing decade the population grew (a high of 82,000 in 1930), machine shops and foundries expanded, new yards were opened up across the city. *Ripley's Believe It or Not* featured Altoona for having the largest engine house in the world. Altoona was defined by the railroad. "Behold a city," one booster wrote, "bustling with industry . . . alive to twentieth-century methods . . . one of the finest of all the hives of industry on earth."

The core of Altoona was laid out as a grid with the railroad tracks running through the town, between 9th and 10th Avenues. Tenth Avenue and beyond included the business district—where my parents had their restaurant—and continued upward toward housing for the professional classes. Ninth Avenue on down was where many of the railroad workers lived. The east side of the shop yards, the wrong side of the tracks. My grandmother's first house was right on 9th Avenue, and every morning she would sweep the soot from her door.

My grandfather was employed by the railroad as a basic laborer, cleaning waste and debris, hauling materials, coupling and uncoupling freight cars. It was hard and dangerous work, and not long into the job he lost his leg in a gruesome accident. Still, when they were old enough, my uncles took jobs with the railroad as well. It was what you did.

Many of the men in the yards were immigrants—from Southern Italy, Eastern Europe, or Russia—or the sons of immigrants, German and Irish. At the end of the day, they walked back east of the yards. Each ethnic group had its neighborhood, and though the Italians tended to settle on streets with others from the same region of their home country, they formed a robust, if rivalrous, Little Italy. There were markets and meat shops, bakeries and beauty parlors, the Banco Italiano, Santella's Funeral Home, the Crown of Italy.

This history predates my birth, but I do have a sense of that immigrant community, a feeling speckled with people and objects. There is Phillip the barber, one chair in his shop, and Zia Carmella, the good witch who anointed me against the evil eye before we left Altoona. There was a little market across the street from my grandmother's house that had candy in glass jars. And there was my grandmother's house itself, shaded rooms with dark wood, a much-trafficked kitchen, large pots on the stove, boiling, a slamming screen door, peppers hanging on the back porch—and that garden, the vines and cornstalks, the chickens. My grandmother, Frances Meraglio, is very clear in these memories, short, heavyset, walking with a hobble, dark print dresses with light flowers, full of affection for me.

These memories blend with old photographs and with stories told by my mother, by my uncles and aunts, told again and again until, over time, they expand memory, flesh it out, make me wonder if, in fact, I was *there*. My mother, a young girl in torn leggings, clambering up the fence of the shop yards to wave at her father. Carmen Melico, vaulting into my grandmother's yard in a dead sprint to escape his brother Bruno's blazing shotgun. My grandparents dancing the tarantella at the Crown of Italy. My grandfather looking up as the ash pan is slipping loose from the crane. My father introducing himself to my mother at the diner called Tom and Joe's.

The stories were full of characters and dramatic events—tragic or comic—and exaggerated gesture. My folks would speak in accents, add sound effects, look heavenward at the climax. Nothing was commonplace in the telling. I came at an early age to expect in people a little flair, in events a rise and fall. All of us—from wartime mayor Charlie Rhodes, to Grandma, to the guy who hauled ashes through the neighborhood—we all merit an extra stroke of the brush.

Before one of my visits, a friend gave me a notebook, one of those little blank books. I filled it. Notes in a diner, early in the morning on my aunt's porch, in wobbly script walking toward the tracks. After that, I brought a notebook with me on every trip.

I copied down the stories my uncles told about the old days and old timers, trying to capture the things they did with their voices and their hands. I recorded the place names (Zanesville, Zelienople) and roadside attractions (from the Croatian Hall to the Blue Spruce Motel) as we drove through western Pennsylvania and into Ohio and back, following the routes my uncles and aunts and so many others took as they looked for work, the railroad laying people off, the auto industry booming. And I made lists—lots of lists—of chipped trophies and photos and broken furniture stored in attics; of knick-knacks in china cabinets (a shot glass "Just a swallow from Capistrano," a little mail truck, a plaster pieta); of city landscapes, grass through cracks in concrete, debris in vacant lots, hand-lettered signs and items for sale in dusty storefront shops.

Once back in Los Angeles, I'd turn the notes into fuller descriptions, scenes, sometimes a poem. There was an alcove over the stairs that led up to my front door. It had windows on three sides, one that opened to an ocean breeze. I had a small desk in it, one my mother bought for me when I entered high school, and some books, a dictionary, a thesaurus, and lots of hanging plants. My place was in the rear of the lot, back off the street, so it was quiet, sunny, and I'd lose myself in the notebooks, the landscape and stories and memories of the first city that I knew.

Here's a passage from that walk down to the railroad tracks, converted in the alcove from notebook to vignette:

> Before this visit I had the sense that Altoona was a city with a palette of grays and dirty white. Maybe it was darker, more metallic when I was a child and the railroad was going strong. Or maybe I got that impression from my mother's photographs of the city, black and white and mostly taken around the restaurant: people smiling against a backdrop of brick and iron and dim store facades. What catches me now is how lush everything is. Altoona is dense with vegetation. It is also hilly . . . and

humid. Walking toward the railroad, the pavement angles down, then evens out, then rises as high as forty degrees. Other streets descend rapidly into brief valleys. The walk is quiet and luxuriant, a damp heat, an occasional leaf-turning breeze—the sudden appearance of a rising brick street or a little valley, homes and churches in the recess below.

Halfway to the tracks, I start to notice the difference in the homes . . . and the streets. This is the older section on the good side of the tracks, once well off, now not well off at all. Tree roots jam through the brick and concrete sidewalks, grass and a weed that looks almost like romaine lettuce—it might be dandelion—spread out over the crevices to make the streets green and soft, almost tropical. At least one house on any given block is vacant and any given block has at least one empty lot, rich with ivy, sumac, and something my cousin calls "blueweed." One lot has an old stove on its side, the oven door open and bent. A dilapidated wooden stairway rises to another lot, the final step leading to air and tall grass. It is covered with morning glories. I get a strong whiff of jasmine—or is it gardenia?—as I walk by. Everything is still and close and clear to the eye. I go up the stairway—careful . . . it wavers but holds me—and look down the other side of the lot into one of the valleys. It has the slight shimmer of a mirage, yet what I can see is somehow precise and stationary. It's as if the angle, the heat, and the silence create an alternative optics that keeps the valley safely distant while allowing the fine detail of a set piece: a dark spire, two blue shirts on a clothesline, a tree with cream flowers, phone poles, antennas, and sharp gables. The particulars of the community are stripped of whatever love or cruelty you'd find there; you are given instead the flowering tree, the peak of a house, the shirt on the line.

There is something lovely about being alone with the past. Things look smaller, or larger, than you recall. Feeling and further memory rush in unexpectedly. Simple objects are vibrant with meaning. Even the most outgoing soul drifts into reflection. It's all so personal, so much a part of where and who you once were, private, of another time, but right around the corner in recollection.

Here is another moment from that walk through Altoona, up to the front door of our old house:

I walk over to my house and up the stairs. I cup my hand and look in the front door—it's half glass now . . . was it always?—knock, and no one answers. It's a doctor's office, but there's that staircase to the second floor where we lived. The staircase, my God. I lean my head against the glass as a strange memory comes to me. I am sitting on the bottom step of the staircase, sobbing and shaking. Some big kid I didn't know had kicked me in the stomach and ran off. My mother is holding my legs, rubbing them, silent, looking right at me, as somber as I've ever seen her. I try the door. It's the outer door, I see as I walk in, to two offices. The eye doctor is to the right, on the first floor—he's closed—and there's a hearing aid repair upstairs. It smells old—the wood, the rug running up the stairs. Like a chest of old clothes. The banister is worn dull, and it's smooth to the touch. *Here goes.* I would run up these stairs and turn right to my favorite room—the others are less distinct at this moment—to my parents' bedroom. The mysterious room where the adults lived. Drawers with things hidden under shirts. Tall places I couldn't reach. An armoire with little doors. A big, big closet. I'd sneak into the closet, my face reaching somewhere about the knee of hanging suits and dresses, and whirl around.

The Parents' Closet

Brush your cheeks
along your mother's dresses,
your arms along
your father's tweeds.
Open drawers.
Run your hands
through scarves and hankies.
Look down.
Wiggle your toes
into a huge brogan.
Turn and turn

in the hanging fiber.
Oh, to be grown up.
Oh, to be so richly textured.

My mother, father, and I were the first of the family to leave Altoona.
It was the early 1950s, and the Pennsylvania Railroad was beginning
its long decline. As the railroad failed, so did all the businesses in
Altoona, including the Rose Spaghetti House. Some of my younger
uncles would also leave, following the lure of General Motors to Ohio,
then to Michigan. My grandmother stayed in that house with the garden. My aunt Jenny and her husband Eddie moved to the outskirts of
town, to semirural Newry where Eddie would become postmaster,
and Jenny, fresh from the Rose Spaghetti House, would open a small
diner alongside the post office. My uncle Frank, the oldest of the boys,
stayed in Altoona, stuck it out with the railroad, and raised his family
about fifteen blocks from my grandmother's house. He went there
every day after work to care for her until she died.

Sometimes on our visits to Altoona, my mother and I would split
up in the evenings, each of us staying with a different relative, she, let's
say, with her mother or her sister, and me with my cousin or with
Uncle Frank.

I liked spending time at Frank's. My mother and I lived there right
before we moved to L.A., my father already on the West Coast trying
to find a home. I remember a triangular room upstairs stacked with
mattresses where I slept, and outside that room the small door to the
beckoning attic where, I could see from outside, pillow cases hung
over the windows. There was the bathroom with a claw-footed tub
and a large, red enema bag on the back of the door. And I remember
to this day a scene from Frank's early TV where a ghostly figure walks
through a wall, scaring me for days.

Frank was a thick-chested man with big, powerful hands, olive
skin, black hair combed straight back. He wore glasses with a heavy,
dark frame that gave him a scholarly look. And he had a scholar's temperament. He read up on things. He knew the history of the railroad,
the generations of engines and freight cars, the technological innova-
tions. He was drawn to nineteenth-century American poetry and
memorized it. He observed the world around him, wrote long letters

in neat script, full of detail and easy humor. I have one written in the mid-1950s to his sister Jenny in which he quotes "The Vision of Sir Launfal" ("Down swept the chill winds . . .") to describe the weather in Altoona and later rhapsodizes about a car trip he took when visiting us in L.A., from the sun setting over the beach in Santa Monica to the multicolored neon along Wilshire Boulevard's Miracle Mile.

Frank retired from the railroad. All his children are gone and his wife is dead, her clothes still hanging in an armoire in their bedroom. He sees a lot of friends from the old days. And he has new passions—golf and gardening—which he studies. The local nursery sends him to talk to gardening groups about growing roses.

After I arrive at Frank's, we spend some time in his garden. The roses are in full bloom—yellow, pink, red, dappled—the fragrance staying with me even after we walk back into the house.

We settle in at the table in the kitchen, and Frank asks about poker. Tonight it's poker. He splashes plastic chips across the table and deals the cards. Two hands. The two of us play late into the night.

And with the cards come stories.

Frank talks about his mother, about the immigrants and old Altoona, about bootleggers, and street toughs, and petty criminals. He slides a loaf of bread and a plate of cold cuts—ham, salami—toward me.

Frances Meraglio, Frank's mother, my grandmother, looms large this evening as she usually does in our family lore. I knew her when she was older, not well, slow-moving. But in the stories she emerges as fierce and indomitable, holding tight rein on the family—slapping the girls for wearing lipstick, taking a broom handle to the boys for gambling—and at the same time furiously protecting them from poverty, the mean streets, and the law.

Sammy was the second youngest of her sons, a sweet-natured guy with a yen for liquor and gambling, sickly as a child, so skinny that everyone called him Herk, short for Hercules. He died young, after heart surgery.

Sammy ran a pool hall from where he peddled illegal lottery tickets. One night, the constable, a local boy who had eaten at my grandmother's table, comes to the house to serve Sammy a warrant for his arrest. He hems and haws and tries to explain what he is doing, and why he has to do it, and how bad doing it makes him feel. Frank pauses: *Imagine your grandmother listening to this.* Wait a minute, she says. She turns and reaches behind the door for the broom. She had been boiling water for spaghetti. Her eye catches the pan on the stove. That seems like a good idea, too. She lunges through the door in a rage, and I can see the constable stumbling backward, thick in his steaming overcoat, Frances slapping him with the broom out into the street. When Sammy finally came home, tipsy and singing, he got the broom as well, though, thank God, he was spared the hot water. Frank laughs, "Your uncle Herk, rest his soul, did get arrested once, and when Mom went to bail him out, he begged the jailer not to release him!"

In equal measure to tales of my grandmother's ferocity are stories that celebrate her intelligence and cunning. A story typically begins with a version of "You know, your grandmother couldn't read or write and she had no education, but . . ." Frank deals another hand and tells the story about the popcorn truck.

When she was older, Frances bought a popcorn truck. She pressed into service my aunt Jenny, and uncle Frank and his kids, and any of my other uncles who hadn't yet moved to Ohio. My mother, father, and I were in L.A. by this time, but when we'd visit Altoona, I'd see large pots of red candy for candied apples bubbling like lava on my grandmother's stove. (The same pot that baptized the constable?) The truck was a compact box of a thing, and as Frank talks, I remember standing in it fascinated with the cotton candy machine, spinning pink sugar gossamer. Grandma would take the truck to ballgames or auto races or the fairground, where, for ten percent of her gross, she could do business. Frank describes a hectic day.

"The money was coming in so fast, we had to throw it on the floor. Five-dollar bills. Tens." The crew worked like crazy for hours while Frances popped more corn and spun more cotton candy. She was also snatching the bills from beneath everyone's feet and stuffing them in her big, black shoes. By the end of the night, there was a truckload of exhausted people and a bag of peanuts or two smashed underfoot. "Hey, Mom," Jenny asked, "how'd we do?" "Eh, not so good. Maybe $60.00. Give the man $6.00." "Now Mom was no fool," Frank observes. She knew that the ground owner could gauge her business by the amount of debris around the truck, so she sent Frank's kids out to collect and ditch popcorn boxes and peanut bags. On the way home everyone was too beat to talk . . . except Frances, who complained that her feet hurt.

If the stories about my grandmother celebrated her mighty determination and wiliness, the stories about Altoona's characters and small-time crooks were more vaudeville and Marx Brothers, entertainment Frank saw in his youth that blended with what he heard and saw on the street. A mix of irony and pratfall. You can almost hear the crack of the drum at the climax.

There were the bootlegging brothers, Henry and Monk, from Gallitzin, a small town in the Allegheny Mountains outside Altoona. These guys had a chicken farm as a front, the still hidden in a shed among the hens and roosters. It seems that the brothers would dump the mash into a nearby creek. But as luck would have it, the creek dried up one summer and the chickens ate the mash—two hundred drunk, flapping chickens running across the farm, a sure tip-off to the federal agents swarming the hills.

Then there was the time Monk took an empty car down Sugar Run Road to find out where the feds had set their roadblocks. Sure enough, the car is stopped. And there's Monk, cocky, big talker, smug as the agent opens the trunk. But the many loads of grain had left seeds throughout the crevices of the trunk bed, all sprouting nicely. "What's that?" the agent asks, waving another agent over. "Uh, I d-dunno," stammers Monk. "And Mickey," Frank laughs, "God looked down and shook his head."

My grandmother played her small part in this Prohibition saga. After her husband lost his leg, she started making wine and beer in her cellar. My mother and her sister Jenny helped out, corking and capping the bottles at the end of the process. Frank remembers the bottles going off at night, fermentation out of control, the dog, Jesse, barking at the random popping.

Grandma didn't have the equipment or space and shelter to make hard liquor, so she got that from Gallitzin, possibly carried by the hapless Henry and Monk. Frank describes guys coming to the back door in heavy overcoats—winter and summer—water bottles filled with booze hanging from ropes over their shoulders like provolone in an Italian market. And here Frank lays down his cards and walks flat-footed across the kitchen floor, shoulders stooped with imaginary whiskey.

These stories had been shaped over the years, in the stockyards, in crap games, in Uncle Sammy's pool hall, in Phillip's Barber Shop—

now told again to a new generation of listeners. If another brother were present, Frank would turn to him for confirmation, handing off the narrative baton. I'd heard many of the stories before, especially about Grandma's bootlegging, but no matter. I loved the performance of it all: the rise and fall of the voice, the accented English or all the "dis" and "dat" talk, the widening of the eyes in mock surprise, the dramatic use of the body. My uncles were attuned to foible and mishap, and thus their tales of crime and violence often had a "Gang That Couldn't Shoot Straight" quality to them. Sometimes literally.

One of Frank's cousins, let's call him Angelo, a guy with bad eyesight and equally bad judgment, found out that his wife was cheating on him. So one day Angelo comes home early, parks his car down the street, and goes to the back fence. "Hey, my good friend," he calls to the startled neighbor, "come out here. I have something for you." When the guy appears, Angelo pulls out a .22 and starts shooting. Now here Frank would hold up his hand and remind us, "bad eyes." Angelo shoots four times at the neighbor, who is frozen in fear, and misses every time. Finally, the guy comes to his senses and jumps sideways—whereupon Angelo's fifth bullet hits him square in the knee. "Hell," Frank observes, "if the guy'd a stood still, he'd a never got hit!"

I would come back to Los Angeles full of such stories, eager to tell them. Some of my friends enjoyed them, but others—a teacher, a psychologist—were shocked at the violence, which was too disturbing to be funny.

Maybe I wasn't telling the stories right. Maybe you had to be there. My friends' reaction caught me off guard, unsettled me—a figure-ground reversal that brought violence into focus. The beatings Grandma gave her kids would today get her charged with child abuse. God knows who Henry and Monk roughed up, or worse, as part of their bootlegging enterprise. Some stories had as backdrop the violations of the street or the organized crime that the booming railroad—all that payroll cash—brought to Altoona. Interethnic rivalry—Germans, Irish, Italians—flared into assault. And then there's that poor guy who Angelo left with a shattered kneecap.

My family grew up in a violent world, and the reaction in Los Angeles drove that home. I had to take Altoona to L.A. to see it. But the reaction also got me to thinking harder about what my uncles did with their world as they narrated it.

Just as much as I liked to hear stories about the past, my uncles clearly liked to tell them. The pleasure of performance. There is, as well, the passing on of their history, certain things about that history that they don't want forgotten, that are emphasized by the format of the stories. I got to know my grandmother as young and powerful, and the children of my cousins, people who never knew Frances Meraglio, talk about her now in ways that highlight her shrewd intelligence. "You know, Grandma couldn't read or write, but. . . ." And the telling and retelling of the stories provided my folks with the opportunity to reminisce, to speak their memories together. It was common on the car rides from Pennsylvania to Ohio and back—one of my uncles driving—for my mother or Aunt Jenny to start in, to ask for the story of so-and-so, for my sake, but, I think, to hear it again, to laugh again, or to add a detail or two, and then to pick up a thread and start in on another one.

What is revealing, though, is that outside the borders of the stories— sometimes within minutes of the telling—the statements about the old days were often sober and stark: the layoffs, the struggle to survive, the aching desire for a better life. I remember walking with my mother through her old neighborhood. A tattered curtain fluttered out of the house next to the dilapidated Crown of Italy. "We used to live like that," she said. "So poor."

The past is not denied in the stories—people struggle and suffer and are hemmed in—but the tragic is slanted for its comedy or to make a point about surviving in hard times. The performance is hugely important here. The turn of the head, the pitch of the voice, if just for the moment, cast a different light on hardship. The dead are present in Altoona, in funeral photographs, the casket open, in old dresses hanging in an armoire, but they're present, too, in the stories, animated with their own stories to tell. And everyone has a story. I sit with them in the alcove over my front stairs, my own curtain fluttering out the window.

Ella: Family Stories, Family Secrets

Rebecca Blevins Faery

Rebecca Blevins Faery is an essayist, poet, and literary scholar whose work has been published in a wide variety of journals. She is the author of Cartographies of Desire: Captivity, Race, and Sex in the Shaping of an American Nation *and, with Carl Klaus and Chris Anderson, of the anthology* In Depth: Essayists for Our Time. *She directs the first-year writing program at the Massachusetts Institute of Technology where she teaches beginning and advanced courses in creative nonfiction.*

1. Missing Woman

Who was she? When she left, what was she thinking? Where did she go, and why?

Here is what I know: She was very beautiful. Her hair was the blackest black, and so were her eyes. She was born Ella Seagroves in Huntsville, Alabama, probably in the mid-1880s. She had a sister named Nettie, and a brother, too, I think, though I remember that only vaguely, and his name not at all. I don't remember ever hearing anything about her father. Her dark beauty caught the eye of my great-grandfather, Will Ragsdale, when she was still very young. So, for that matter, was he. They must have married sometime around 1901 or 1902, when Will would have been twenty or twenty-one and Ella still in her teens. Probably those ages weren't all that unusual for marriage, especially among poor people, in those days. I don't know how they met, though surely I was told the story by Grandpa, who so loved to tell me stories about his childhood and youth when I was small. Perhaps her father or brother was a millworker like Will; the 1890 census in Huntsville lists four men named Seagroves who were mill employees.

But however they met, they did marry, and their son Lonnie, my mother's father, "Pop" to me, was born in 1903. Not long after that—I think in 1906, when Ella would have been maybe twenty-one or so—while Will was at work at the cotton mill one day, she cleaned the house to its usual spotlessness and she bathed little Lonnie, three at the time, and dressed him in clean clothes and took him to a neighbor's. When Will came home she was gone, without a word, and without a trace.

I come from several generations of first children who married young, and my great-grandfather was only fifty-nine when I was born. Lonnie, my mother's father, was only eighteen when my mother was born. Her mother, Elyse Wilhoite, was five years older than Lonnie. My mother married at eighteen and I was born when she was nineteen.

My great-grandfather was probably the most significant person in my early life. He retired from the cotton mill in Chattanooga, where I was born, when I was six, and after we moved first to Alabama and then to Virginia, he spent most winters with us, being my "pupil" when I wanted to play school and was the teacher, my "customer" when I wanted to play store and was the storekeeper, taking me to Saturday movie matinees every week. One of the family photographs I most cherish is of five generations of us: Grandpa, Pop, my mother, me, my two children. People are astonished when I tell them that my great-grandfather lived until I was almost thirty and knew my children. And it *is* astonishing, given the late marriages and later child-bearings that are the norm today.

I saw Ella's mother and her sister Nettie once, when I was eight and my parents, great-grandfather, and I visited Huntsville in the summer of 1948. I think the Alabama State Fair was in Huntsville at the time because I have a vague memory of going to the fair on the same visit, of the sticky cotton candy I loved and the thrilling rides like Crack-the-Whip and the voices of midway barkers luring passersby in to see the "freaks"—the Fattest Woman in the World, the Wild Man of Borneo, the Bearded Lady, the Hermaphrodite (for adults only).

My great-grandfather, my beloved Grandpa, was sixty-seven that year. He had wanted to go to Huntsville to see his mother-in-law, Grandma Seagroves—Ella's mother. My great-grandfather visiting his mother-in-law! And I was there, a long-legged, awkward, and dreamy child. Nettie was there too; she took care of, cared for, her mother, who was old and bedridden and blind.

It was high summer, and the Alabama heat was oppressive and sticky, making us all listless and intensifying the odors of the house— dust, the ghostly residues of cooking, the sweat and scent of old clothes, old furniture, bodies. In Grandma Seagroves' bedroom the yellowed paper window shades were drawn against the summer heat. The room was dim and smelled of stale urine. A pale and moulty canary, its cage hung on a tall stand near the bed, was very still and peered fixedly at us visitors, though with little interest. Grandma Seagroves, with Nettie's help, struggled to a sitting position on the side of the bed, the better to be sociable. She was a bulky woman, dressed in some sort of wrapper, thin and dark, over her nightgown. Her blind eyes were rheumy and streaked with yellow. Long wisps of thin gray hair escaped from combs and floated around her head and shoulders. She wanted to touch me, pet me—her great-great-granddaughter, the latest twig of Ella's tree. She smiled wanly but with evident great pleasure and groped for me. I shrank back against my mother, embarrassing all of us, but the old woman's odor dizzied me and I was afraid of her. My mother's great-grandmother. My great-great-grandmother.

Her daughter Ella having been born, as well as I can figure, in the mid-1880s, Grandma Seagroves must have been born sometime in the 1860s, so would have been in her eighties that year of our visit. I was eight, my young mother twenty-seven, my great-grandfather— my mother's grandfather—sixty-seven.

Nettie was old, too, as far as I was concerned—probably in her mid sixties. I don't know if Ella was older or younger than Nettie; they must have been close in age. I don't know if Nettie ever married. That day she smiled and patted me. Uncomfortable with familiar caresses from a stranger, fearing the imminent crush of an embrace, I stayed on the move, slipping and sliding away from her. But I was curious, too. Grandpa had told me about Nettie, and I had always felt an odd fascination with her name. No one else I knew was named Nettie. Possibly it was a nickname, but for what? Jeanette, maybe? Or Antoinette perhaps, a name that seems somehow too exotic for the family I remember. Now, seeing her for the first time, I stared at her hair. Short, gray, tightly curled. Her name suggested "hairnet" to me, and sure enough, she wore one: soft gray, delicate as a spider's web, it restrained her tight gray curls with unspeakable, nearly invisible tenderness; the merest shadow of boundary lay at Nettie's hairline, and the wispy force of the net gathered itself at her widow's peak into an infinitesimal knot. I remember her smiles, some iced tea with not enough ice and with lemon wedges bobbing in the glasses. I remember all of us standing around in the living room of the dim house, its shades and curtains also drawn against the heat. Grandma Seagroves didn't leave her bedroom. It was understood, I think, that she hadn't long to live, so that this visit would be the last time Grandpa and my mother would see her.

I don't remember much about the house, except that it was small and white, that the furniture was dark, that dust motes danced in the rays of sunlight that made their way in through holes in the curtains or cracks in the shades. A white picket fence surrounded the yard, but some pickets were missing and the fence wanted a fresh coat of paint. I can't recall much about the neighborhood, either, though I can see in my mind's eye that the adjacent houses were surrounded by overgrown trees and shrubs, and I saw that black families occupied a few of the nearby houses. The neighborhood as I remember it—though I couldn't have said this then, wouldn't have understood it—was well past whatever gentility it had once had, the whole area in decline, in the way of old working-class neighborhoods near the hearts of Southern cities. Green and white metal awnings, flecked with rust, curved over the front windows. (Keeping what out? Keeping what in?)

Ella was a vivid absence that day, though no one spoke of her, at least not in my hearing: the wayward daughter/sister/wife/mother who, by skipping out, had made herself more troublingly visible than she ever could have been if she had stayed in the traces. She was the knot holding this tangled skein of kinship together. Grandma Seagroves' lost daughter. Nettie's lost sister. Grandpa's lost wife. Lonnie's lost mother. My mother's grandmother, my great-grand-mother. Great. Grand. Mother. Her coal-black hair and eyes.

Grandpa's hair had been black too, I'd been told. Now it was almost white. But their son Lonnie's hair was dark brown, thick and kinky, and my mother's hair lighter brown, almost blonde, and thick and wavy. My hair was dark blonde, very thick, and in my childhood "straight as a stick," as my mother used to complain. Shorter pieces stuck out like bristles from the tight braids my mother plaited in my hair each morning. When I was eleven or twelve and on the threshold of womanhood, it began to curl, at first softly around my temples, then finally in waves that turned to ringlets in damp weather. We grow paler and more tame, it seems, our coloring more subdued and our hair less unruly, with each passing generation.

2. Dowd

As I grew older and Grandpa deemed me ready to hear more about Ella, he gave me a few more details about her story, as many as he had to give, I suppose, and they were precious few. Only after I was a married woman did he tell me, sitting at my mother's kitchen table one winter afternoon when the two of us were alone in the kitchen, about trying desperately to find Ella, finding and following traces of her from town to city all over the South. He finally traced her to Memphis somehow, and, leaving Lonnie with Grandma Seagroves, went there to find her. The address he had been given turned out to be a "dowdy house," he said with tears in his eyes even then, more than half a century later. A *dowdy house*, I guess, was his term for a house of prostitution. He waited there in the shadows outside the house for her to come out or come home. He knew she was there or would return, though I don't know how he knew. Finally, late in the evening, he heard a laugh he recognized as hers and watched her coming down the street on the arm of a "fancy man," he told me, perhaps a gambler from the riverboats. Will stepped out of the shadows; Ella stopped in her tracks, her laughter stilled. "I've come to take you home," he said. She tossed her black curls, froze her features, and said to the fancy man, "I never saw this man before in my life." And turned away and walked into the house with her companion.

Years afterward (I don't know how many years, though probably fewer than ten, because this happened before the war began in 1914), Will heard that she was back in Alabama, had "taken up with a railroad man," he told me, and was dying. Probably it was tuberculosis, the great killer in those days of poor Southern folks. Will sent word that he wanted to come see her once more and to bring Lonnie with him: "Tell her that her husband wants to see her," he'd said. She sent word back: the railroad man was her husband now, she said; she had no call to see anybody else. And she died without Will or Lonnie ever seeing her again.

He never got over the pain. Never married again. Sitting at my mother's kitchen table that winter afternoon sometime in the late 1960s, Grandpa told me the story, more than half a century after it happened, and tears rolled down the creases in his cheeks. The freshness of his anguish astonished me. Ella had broken his heart when she left, and it had never healed. He loved her at that moment as much as he had ever loved her, with all the power of his great loving heart.

Oh, she was a bad woman, all right, everyone in my family knew that, though Will never said it, never said anything at all to cast a shadow on her. He just shared the mystery of her disappearance with me. Somehow I understood the regret and guilt he felt but couldn't repair; he never knew, never had a chance to find out, just what had gone wrong and why. He never told my mother about finding Ella in the dowdy house, perhaps because he didn't want to hurt her, or didn't want Lonnie to find out that his mother had been a "fancy woman." Lord knows Lonnie had troubles enough without being told that, his own young wife dead of tuberculosis, leaving him with a three-year-old daughter, my mother, and a son not yet two. A second marriage to a good hardworking woman who had a son, and then together three more children. And all the time the drinking, and other women. Most of all the emotional damage and distance, the tensions that built in him and sometimes erupted in frightening displays of rage and violence. All the while, though, he held down his job as a letter carrier for the post office and fed his large family through the Depression. Thinking about it now, I wonder if he knew what had become of his mother. Even if Will never told him, there were others, Nettie, and Ella's mother. Probably they heard the story from Grandpa, and Lonnie would have been all ears for stories about his lost mother. Maybe, if he had heard the stories, even whispers, when years later the demons of drink and lust drew him, he figured he had it in him. It was his mother, showing up again at last.

Still, even if he didn't know about where Will had found her in Memphis, everybody knew she was a bad woman because she had left her child, and everybody, including me, knew that was the worst thing a woman could ever do. Lonnie, Pop to me, had grown up motherless. Sometimes, when he was small, he stayed in Huntsville with Nettie and Grandma Seagroves while his father moved around the South from mill to mill, always looking for better work. And sometimes, when he was older, Will took Lonnie with him to the new jobs in the new mills. They'd live in boarding houses where they shared a room and took their meals at the common table. I don't know who looked after Lonnie while Will was at the mill. Will knew about being a motherless child; he'd been one himself, because his own mother had died in childbirth with his younger brother Artie when Will was not yet two. He didn't remember his mother at all. So he lavished on his only child all the love he himself as a child had needed so much but never had.

Probably that's why it had been so important to him that Ella be a good mother to Lonnie. And I guess she was a good mother, for as long as she was there. A picture of Lonnie when he was a baby shows him dressed in white ruffles, shoes, a cap. He looks every inch the petted darling.

So what lured or wrenched her away? Was it romance? Love? Lust? Or something else—some secret that helps to explain her dowdy house adventure? Some news she got, some awful surprise? Or someone threatening to reveal a secret she had kept buried, hidden from her husband, a secret too terrible to be known without destroying the life they had built together?

3. Aporia

Here's what I don't know, what I want to know, but what I can never know: Why did she leave? It is a hole, a gap in my family history, one that can never be filled with facts, so my imagination has been drawn to it all these years. It's a hole I must try to fill with speculations, with *stories*. Why she left, where she went, are questions I've asked myself again and again about this woman whose genes I carry within me, from whom I have perhaps inherited some traits. After all, I've skipped out on husbands too, two of them, though not so abruptly, and not without warning. And I didn't leave my children behind, would never, ever have done so.

One story, an obvious possibility to be found also in fictional characters like Madame Bovary, Anna Karenina, and countless others, is that she sought and found romance. She had, after all, married very young, probably too young. Led by the feeling so poignantly expressed many years later in Peggy Lee's song "Is That All There Is?"—a question I came to ask myself too, long years after her death—perhaps she could not imagine living out her life as the wife of a poor millworker and the mother of a small boy. Did she have a lover, someone who promised her the excitement her respectable life lacked? Had some handsome man waltzed by one day and stolen her heart? Grandpa had told me she was vain of her beauty, and she loved to get dressed up and go out. She dressed her dark curls and enlisted her husband's help in lacing her stays tighter and tighter to make her waist tiny; he objected, and they argued. It couldn't be healthy, he said, to lace yourself up like that so you scarce could breathe. And besides, it was unseemly for a married lady. No doubt her exhibitions of vanity frightened him.

They argued, too, about what Ella did all day while he was working at the mill. He told me this with great sadness all those many years later after he had retired from the mill and stayed home all day and started helping his daughter-in-law, Lonnie's wife, with the housework. The house had always looked the same to him, he said; it just never occurred to him how much work it took to keep it looking that way until so many years later when he was home all day and found out. He wished, I could tell, that he had understood then, when it mattered; he wished he could tell Ella that now he knew how hard she had worked to keep the house looking always clean and neat as a pin, how much he now appreciated how hard she must have worked. But it was too late.

Maybe she was a woman who chafed at the limitations imposed on women of her day. What options did she have for a larger life? Maybe her vanity was one way she could imagine of gaining some kind of power, the power of a beautiful woman over men. Maybe, when men looked at her with desire, or promised something better than what she had, she felt the rush of being in charge. It might have been the only way she knew to escape the confines of her narrow domestic and marital life. If she left home, husband, and child for love, her shame must have been profound when she was abandoned and need drove her to use her beauty, her body, to stay alive. At times when desire has led me into deep waters, this is the story of her disappearance and what I know of her fate that has felt the most convincing to me.

At other times, when I chafed at the confinements of my life as just a wife and mother (though motherhood has been the greatest joy of my life), when I longed for something more, something better, when I imagined other possibilities for myself, I've thought of Ella. Maybe she would have chosen a different path for herself if she could have; maybe she would be glad for the expanded possibilities I had and finally claimed for myself. If that was the case, Ella's resistance to her woman's role came to full flower in me, when second-wave feminism caught me up and shaped me into the passionate feminist scholar and teacher I am today.

But that is not the only story I have imagined.

Another story: As in all families, there were subtexts in mine, things that were occasionally spoken obliquely, whispered occasionally, but never openly acknowledged and accepted. One was that my great-grandfather Will was Indian. I assume he was only part Indian because of his blue eyes, though there are a great many blue-eyed Indians now, and there have been for a very long time, since romantic and sexual liaisons between Indians and English colonizers began in the seventeenth century. I don't know if his Indian ancestry came through his father's line or his mother's. I don't know which tribal group he came from. Maybe none of that is important. What is clear is that no one in my family embraced that part of our heritage and identity. There were small signs, such as Lonnie teasing his father by calling him "Big Chief Sore-Tail" whenever Grandpa was quietly cross about something or other, probably Lonnie's bad behavior. And then there were the prominent cheekbones, Grandpa's and Lonnie's, and Lonnie's olive-ruddy skin, which turned up two generations later in my brother too.

It is a fact that anyone whose origins are in the Deep South and who has Indian ancestry is likely also to have some black ancestry. Indian communities from the early years of European colonization welcomed runaway slaves, intermarried with them, assimilated them fully into the tribal group. William Loren Katz takes up the relatedness of the nation's two racial outsider groups in his book *Black Indians: A Hidden Heritage*. And that, of course—I realized this only ten or fifteen years ago—is the reason my family, deeply Southern and thus carrying in its baggage all the prejudices common to the South, never talked about Grandpa's Indian "blood." Being white was too important.

These days, Indian wannabes proliferate, people take pride in having Indian ancestry, so that even my mother, who valued respectability above all else, began to talk openly in the last years of her life about Grandpa's being part Indian. And to think of him as a little Indian boy goes a long way to explain some of his personal history. After his mother's death, an older sister, Elizabeth, cared for her younger brothers, Eddie, Will, and Artie. Their father was a "drummer," Grandpa told me, a traveling salesman, though I don't know what he sold. Elizabeth too died, in a smallpox epidemic when the boys were still young, and their father was forced to farm the boys out to a childless couple who gave them food and shelter in exchange for work on their farm. And food and shelter was not all they got. The Thors—Grandpa loved to tell stories about the cruelty of "Old Man Thor," as he always called him—were not satisfied to exploit the boys' labor. Thor himself must have been a certifiable sadist. He sent the boys one by one after dark alone into the woods to the well when the cries of the "painter"—panther—that lived in the woods could be heard, just to terrify them, and he succeeded. Whenever one of them displeased him for some trivial reason, he wrapped a rope around the boy's ankles, hoisted him up head down by the rope thrown over the rafters, and beat him with a leather strap until he bled or lost consciousness.

The boys slept in an unheated lean-to, and Eddie, the oldest, contracted a severe cold and earache. Thor provided him no medical attention or care. Will and Artie woke up one morning to find Eddie dead in his bed. The two ran away from the Thor place and survived for a while by sucking raw eggs they stole from people's henhouses. Someone in the town where they ended up—Scottsboro, maybe, where Will and Artie had been born—found out, somehow, that their father had also died. The two little boys were orphans, alone in the world. A preacher and his wife took them in for a while—perhaps a charitable gesture to those "little Indian boys"—cleaned them up, fed them, and sent them to school—the only schooling Will ever had. It was enough to enable him to read and to write, though laboriously. A couple who had no children wanted to adopt Artie, who must have been seven or eight at the time, and he moved with them to Texas. They must not have adopted him legally, though, because his name did not change. The brothers did not see each other again until they were grown. The preacher and his wife who had been housing and feeding the boys moved on, and Will, before he was ten, was on his own, working in one of the textile mills that were becoming so common throughout the South and boarding at a boarding house. He earned, he never tired of telling me, fifty cents a week, and paid a quarter of that for room and board to the lady who ran the boarding house. He worked six days a week, twelve hours a day, this being around 1890, before the passage of child labor laws.

And so, hardworking and honest and tenderhearted despite, or perhaps because of, all his troubles, he grew to be a man, met Ella Seagroves, fell in love, and married. He might have mentioned to her casually at some point his being part Indian; maybe he revealed that part of his history in a moment of unguarded intimacy when he wanted her to know him wholly. Perhaps his mixed-race identity is part of what moved her to reject her husband and child, to flee and to leave her child behind.

Or maybe she had a secret of her own.

Another story, this one more painful but probably equally plausible: Several years ago, when I read for the first time (but not the last) Judson Mitcham's beautiful novel *The Sweet Everlasting*, I stopped dead on page 10 when I read what the narrator, Ellis Burt, a simple white Southern country boy grown to a young man, says about Susan, the woman who becomes his wife, when he sees her for the first time:

> When I looked at Susan that first time, I didn't have a clue, though it's a fact that she could have been a picture in a book. I mean, she stood out right away from everybody around her— blackest hair I'd ever seen on a white woman, and dark eyes.

I knew something right then because that was so like the phrase I'd heard so often from Grandpa when he talked about Ella: "Blackest hair you ever saw on a white woman, black as a blackbird's wing. And the blackest eyes."

In the novel, a few years after their son is born, Susan tells Ellis "the whole truth about some things" and confesses to him that her "daddy was white" and that her "mama [didn't] look colored at all, but she was. Her mama and daddy was supposed to have been real light-skinned, and they say her mama's hair was just like mine."

Ellis writes, "The Bible says we shall all be changed, in the twinkling of an eye." And at that moment, Ellis loses sight of the reality of Susan, this woman he has loved so deeply for years, and the hate-filled racism that permeated the air he breathed as he grew up and lived in the Georgia of the 1940s takes hold of him, and that hateful racist culture speaks through him:

> "You just gonna sit there and just like that you gonna tell me I married a nigger? . . . All these years, and the worst of it— goddamn you to hell, goddamn you—you done made my boy a

nigger too, put your own nigger blood in his veins and made
him a nigger too. *My boy, my boy.*"

Disaster follows; their son ends up dead and Ellis loses Susan. He has
decades to taste the bitter fruit of regret and sorrow. Like Will, sorrow
tempers Ellis, and he becomes a quietly caring and compassionate
man whose only happiness is found in memories of times when he
and Susan and their boy were together.

I've taught this novel for years in my "Writing About Race" class at
MIT. Students love it, and they understand it as an example of the
craziness of the prohibitions against racial mixing. As I tell them, and
as Susan in Mitcham's novel makes clear, the idea of racial "purity" is
just that, an idea, in no way a reality, because all of us are mixed, one
way or another. As Albert Murray has written, "The United States is in
actuality not a nation of black people and white people. It is a nation
of multicolored people. There are white Americans so to speak and
black Americans. But any fool can see that the white people are not
really white, and that black people are not black. They are all interre-
lated one way or another."

Reading and teaching this novel always makes that day in
Huntsville in 1948 rise up vivid in my memory. The black families in
the neighborhood. The slim perch of respectability to which the
Seagroves clung.

And I think of Ella. Maybe a knock came on the door one day
while Will was at work, from someone who had a grudge or a claim
of some sort, someone who had some knowledge of her family history
that could destroy the life she had built, change her child's future. It
was 1906, and Jim Crow was alive and well in the Deep South.
Miscegenation laws were in place and enforced. It only took a drop of
black "blood." If she could pass, and did, who could blame her? What
does being white, or being black, mean anyhow? This is the only version of her story I have imagined that can explain her decision to
abandon her child. And her descent into the oldest profession, her
finding refuge in the dowdy house.

If this version of her story is true, I'm sure Will never knew. And as
I write this, I must say again that I have no facts, just small shreds of
evidence and a lot of speculation. I grew up a blonde and blue-eyed
girl, and I have enjoyed all my life the privileges of whiteness. I don't

want to deny that fact in wondering about the racial history of my family. It is the racial history of countless supposedly white Southern families, after all, whose ancestors hid or denied the forbidden passions that led them to cross the boundaries of race despite the warnings and the dangers. That white slave masters assumed a right of sexual access to the black women they or their friends owned, resulting in a profoundly racially mixed black population in this country, we all know, acknowledge, take for granted. That it sometimes was love and desire that led to racial mixing is a fact too often denied. But that mixing, forced or chosen, is *our* racial history, and as James Baldwin has written, "People are trapped in history and history is trapped in them."

Maybe the real story of Ella Seagroves is a combination of two of the stories I've spun here—a lover who led her astray and away and who left her when he learned her secret. It would have been an easy thing to do. What recourse did she have but to trade on the only asset she then possessed, her beauty? She would have been but one among many women in the brothels along the Mississippi with a trace of black "blood." I weep for the ill will human beings have held toward each other, and for Ella, if a remote fact of family history forced her away from her husband and child and into the arms of fancy men. I'm glad for her if some unknown man cared enough for her, was enchanted enough by her beauty, however tarnished, to take her in and live with her as his wife. The pain of her story, though, is part of my story too and that of my whole family and is with me always, until I breathe my last.

Works Cited

Baldwin, James. "Stranger in the Village," from *Notes of a Native Son*. Boston: Beacon Press, 1955.

Katz, William Loren. *Black Indians: A Hidden Heritage*. New York: Atheneum, 1986.

Mitcham, Judson. *The Sweet Everlasting*. Athens: University of Georgia Press, 1996.

Murray, Albert. *The Omni-Americans: New Perspectives on Black Experience and American Culture*. New York: Outerbridge and Dienstfrey, 1970.

Revealing Secrets,
Writing Poems

Sondra Perl

Sondra Perl spends her academic life writing, teaching writing, and reflecting, often, about both. She has conducted research on how college students write, written books about teachers' lives in the classroom, and recently published a memoir on the way dialogue can lead to reconciliation between the descendants of Nazis and Jews in post–Holocaust Austria. Sondra Perl lives in New York City where she is Professor of English at Lehman College and the Graduate Center of the City University of New York. Her writing of poems is no longer a secret.

oetry always seemed obscure and stuffy to me, the purview of English majors, not what really mattered as I tried to make sense of my life. At least, that's what I thought for most of my adolescence and early adulthood. But as I began to teach writing and then to write, my view of poetry began to change. In writing workshops, I stopped drafting essays and wrote poems instead. I didn't feel particularly skilled, far more the novice than the expert, but I liked what poetry allowed me to do: to reveal a memory by narrowing it to a few telling details, to portray a family member by focusing on a seemingly minor moment, to use something small to say something big. I also discovered that I liked the chiseled quality of poetry, how spare it could be, how the form allowed me to take the sharp edges of my life and turn them into texts.

I didn't think of myself as a poet nor did I think about publishing my poems. My professional writing consisted of articles and books that told stories about teachers and their lives both in and out of the classroom. But privately, especially when something nagged at me or I was feeling unsettled or experiencing a sense of loss or regret, I began to explore my thoughts and emotions by composing poems.

This chapter, then, is itself a revelation: it reveals a kind of writing that for most of my life I have kept private. The poems included here, presented chronologically, are also revealing in another way: they explore moments from my past that, with one exception, were hard for me to live with, moments that called for understanding and clarity, which is one of the reasons I think they emerged as poems. I was, at the moment of composing each one, a writer seeking to understand her life, and as I crafted them, so I also crafted my own knowledge of what was happening to me and around me. What follows, then, is not only a series of revelations about my life and how I think about these events in the present but also a testament to the way the act of writing itself allows for revelations.

The year is 1993. I am living in Riverdale, New York, leading a summer institute for teachers on the teaching of writing. I am married and have three children. I've spent almost all of my life in school, first as a student, then as a teacher, ultimately as a teacher of teachers. My college years are long gone, but somehow, this summer, as I sit with a group of middle and high school teachers, all of us searching for something to write about, I become acutely aware of a memory that lives beneath the surface of my life.

Nose Job

In 1968, my mother and sister checked into
Manhattan Eye and Ear for nose jobs.
My father asked for a package deal:
two for the price of one.
Had I gone too, he would have asked for even more:
three new noses, bumps flattened, curves straightened,
nostrils narrowed,
each cut of the scalpel
eradicating Jewish identity
for a cut rate.

He asked me, teased me, cajoled me,
tried hard to convince me
to go with them:
to have needles inserted up my nostrils
to deaden the pain,
to have the bone broken and reset
so I could be prettier.

My mother and sister had no doubts,
thought it made sense,
this woman's way
to self-improvement.
I couldn't see it,
had a distinct failure of imagination,
couldn't see submitting
to the doctors who would lay me down,
break my nose and reshape it;
to my father who wanted
a better-looking daughter;
to the culture that said
beauty can be bought.

My father and I left them that night,
in their hospital room,
in hospital gowns, and went to see

a play by Harold Pinter. My choice.
He fell asleep as he did the one other time
I asked him to a cultural event. I loved
the starkness of Bergman
and took him, on my college's Father-Daughter weekend,
to see *The Seventh Seal*.
He would have preferred
something lighter, he'd said.

My mother and sister came home,
wore hats in the car.
Covered their faces with chiffon scarves.
Holed up in my mother's bedroom,
in the round bed she shared with my father
and had their meals brought to them on trays.
Came home, eyes red with blood,
skin purpling, faces puffy,
with helmets and straps
to keep the swelling down, to keep
the newly-set bones in place.
Whispered to each other,
finding it hard
to move their jaws.

I wandered the house alone,
wondering at their choice,
their ability to withstand pain,
their desire to be beautiful.
Went to the bathroom mirror, turned sideways,
held up a second mirror,
examined the bump on my nose and
tried to envision
how I would look without it.

Aimlessly I took the car keys.
Made my way to the movies.
Lost myself in Katherine Hepburn's cheekbones

watched as Sir Thomas More gave his life
for what he believed in
and cried.

This is the world I recall when I think of my teens: a world regulated by my mother and father with an overriding focus on surfaces and self-improvement. I escaped it, to some extent, by attending college. It was there that I realized one could improve one's mind instead of one's nose, and while I missed my parents, I didn't miss their desire to reshape my face. I was trying hard, at age twenty, to reshape the path my family had planned for me, to chart something of my own, something I could believe in. I didn't know then how often I would repeat this process.

At the time of the nose jobs, I held my own. I refused to submit. I think now that I was, frankly, as scared of the pain as I was of the potential alteration of my face. But it wasn't easy. I can still recall how restless I felt, wandering the halls of our home, knowing my mother and sister were together, behind closed doors, sharing something I had rejected. But mainly, I was embarrassed. I understood the messages about beauty and selfhood that permeated upper-middle-class culture. I knew, as a female, that a woman was frequently judged by her looks. Certainly, this was the message that had been communicated to me by my mother. And, yes, from time to time, I acquiesced, going to the hair salon in search of a new hairstyle or on special occasions for a manicure and pedicure. But I found the idea of plastic surgery appalling. It seemed so drastic. I just couldn't embrace the pursuit of beauty in the wholehearted way my mother and sister did.

It took over twenty years for me to return to this memory, to begin to explore what it felt like to me at age twenty, a college sophomore, to accompany my mother and sister to the hospital and to be a witness to their desire to become more beautiful. It was hard to acknowledge how unseen I felt as the daughter of a man who seemed to have little interest in the ideas that interested me. But once their bandages were removed and their bruises healed, I returned to college and moved on. I ended up majoring in art history, spending hours in museums, looking carefully at and writing about paintings. I found what I considered to be beautiful, an aesthetic I could admire, an aesthetic that gave me pleasure and that brought me peace. It astounds me now, as I write, that what fascinated me most, what moved me most, were Rembrandt's portraits, the ones that reveal the blemishes and the wrinkles, that expose the signs of aging, rather than hide them. They still do.

A few years later, I am leading a writing workshop for women in my local community. We gather on Monday mornings in my dining room around the large wooden table laden with pens, paper, cake and coffee, and I lead us all in a writing exercise. Sitting there one morning, I glance at the stairs that lead to the second-floor landing and an image of my mother-in-law comes to me. I write this poem:

Bebe

My mother-in-law strides through life
with a forbidding scowl
her nose and breasts protruding
like so much armor,
a three-horned triceratops
ready to defend herself
against attack.

"If you ever divorce,
I'll take his side,"
she once told me
ready as ever
to fend off the imagined hurt
of a failed marriage,
the imagined recriminations of
an ungrateful daughter-in-law,
all of this three years before
we marry.

The owner of a cemetery,
she worked hard, this
mother-in-law of mine,
burying the dead
fighting with the grave-diggers' union,

full of angry black men
who refused to open the earth
on Christmas. She bought
oriental rugs for the bereavement rooms,
planted mums and forsythia and basil
on the grounds of the memorial park
she inherited, the business of burying bodies
passed on from father to daughter.

A tough bird, they called her
those other owners of burial scenes,
the paunchy men off to Miami or Cincinnati
for their annual conventions. Her friends
dressed in dark suits, drank Jack Daniels and
treated her as one of the crowd.

A good sport, she played the game well,
sending her daughter to a junior college,
her son to Harvard. She learned
to order *coquilles St. Jacques*
and to keep her affairs to herself.

Too heavy, with a pacemaker in her
heart, she pants now
as she climbs the stairs
to the guest room.
For three months each year
she visits with us,
reads Dr. Seuss to her grandchildren,
keeps the air conditioning on high,
and occasionally bakes a potato.

On the days I take her shopping,
I'm no longer surprised
when she cocks her head
stares straight into the eyes
of a salesman at Neiman's

and dares him to respond
to her proud claim:
"I'm an old broad, dear.
You can't fool me."

This woman prefers
the company of men,
preferring too
her son to her daughter.
Throughout all the years of childhood,
she drew him close
to those breasts,
tickled his back,
and delighted to see her face
reflected in his.
This woman for whom all men
are objects to charm,
no longer so charming herself,
lives on borrowed breaths
regulated by a machine
buried deep within
the thickening walls of her heart.

As I drive her to the doctor
an irregular heartbeat leaving her faint
I wonder what else lies buried
beneath that skin.

My mother-in-law was as conscious of beauty as were my mother and sister. She cared enormously about her clothes, about the latest styles, about hair and nails and furs and jewelry. But life dealt her a different hand. Unlike my mother and sister, she needed to work to support her family, and she did, for years, own and run a burial ground, a memorial park on the outskirts of Philadelphia, a tough business by anyone's standards. And perhaps it was all those years working in such a hard world that led her to develop, like protective coloring, such strong armor, such a hard exterior.

But, still, as I revisit this poem, written more than a decade ago, I am aware of how many secrets it contains. I realize how little we actually know about people, even those who are close to us. What lies beneath the surface of our skin? I ask. Did I really understand this woman? Over the years, she visited us, living in our house for months at a time. And, slowly, I came to love this woman who loved my children. But did I ever understand what moved her, what touched her, what hurt her or brought her joy?

What strikes me now is the line I never forgot: "If you ever divorce, I'll take his side." When she spoke it to me, we were sitting in a restaurant at the Westbury Hotel on Manhattan's upper east side. It was the first time we were ever alone. Her son, whom I was dating, was working that night, and I naïvely thought that taking her out to dinner by myself would be a caring gesture. In fact, she proceeded to drink too many martinis, and, eyeing me hard, she made that startling pronouncement. Sitting there, I realized that this son of hers had already divorced once, that she had had too much to drink and wanted to protect herself. But still, I was startled by her comment and realized I was out of my depth. What's so strange, of course, is that life plays tricks on us. Years later, her son and I do divorce. She is no longer here to take anyone's side, but I am convinced that if she were, it would be mine.

Another secret about my mother-in-law:

The Bebe Gun

My mother-in-law died
on New Year's Eve.
Alone in a hospital bed
on the Gulf Coast,
she refused food and medication,
closed her eyes and withdrew
from a world grown tired and old.
No more, she said. I choose to go
without a fight, no tears, no final farewells,
not even a simple embrace.
Her final act
an act of refusal.

Her will, always strong,
now bent on dying.

We traveled to Tampa
to dispose of her remains—
this woman who spent her life
burying others
requesting not to be buried.
I spent a day cleaning out
her closet, opening drawers and boxes
filled with lace handkerchiefs
and pennies from 1935.
In the very last box
on the very last shelf
hidden behind a pair of red leather shoes
I found a silver revolver
a .22 in a brown leather case
with a small box of bullets.

I held the gun in my hand,
feeling its weight.
I sighted along its lines
and wondered how to get it home.
I couldn't imagine leaving it there
or carrying it with me on the plane.
I took the gun and slipped it
inside a beaded bag and had
it shipped, committing I imagine an
interstate violation concerning the
transportation of firearms across state lines.

It rests now, this revolver of hers,
among her hats and stockings and photographs,
now on the top shelf of my closet.
I think of it from time to time
and wonder what it must have looked like
in her hand.

This discovery is truly a mystery. My mother-in-law kept a gun in her bedroom closet. Did she ever take it with her when she went, perhaps, on late night calls to a funeral parlor or to the memorial park? Was she afraid, sometimes, of going out on her own? After her husband died, did she fear living alone? Did she fear being attacked? Was the gun a gift from a male admirer who thought she needed protection? Or was it like her diamond ring and her pearl necklace, something to finger, to hold on to, to reassure her that she'd be okay?

Bebe's son also ends up as a mystery to me. In our twenties, when we meet, we spend our vacations traveling. Together we journey to India, Japan, Bali, and Thailand. Drawn to Eastern philosophy, we visit temples and ashrams and imagine that we can partake of the rich traditions of other cultures. At home, once we begin a family, we return to our own religion, Judaism, and raise our children within that tradition as modern, secular Jews. Then, one year, my husband decides he wants to explore the orthodox side of our heritage. I don't understand this desire. I feel unsettled by it, and one night, I try both to describe and understand my shock by composing this poem:

The Return

He dons *talit* and *kipah*
bends from the waist
and prays now
to this God
he claims
to know.

I sit there
watching
bewildered.
Who is this man
I married? Why do I
not recognize him
in his new/ancient garb?

And why do I,
a daughter of Sarah and Rachel,
Ruth and Rebekah
not rejoice
at his spirituality come home
wrapped around him now
like a familiar blanket?

What for years seemed to both of us
silly and old-fashioned
arrogant and rude
stiffnecked and worst of all
embarrassing
he welcomes now with
open arms and heart.

When we smiled smugly
at the earnest young men
in their black hats and *payis*
we knew ourselves to be
modern
and aligned in our new worldedness.
Speakers of romance languages,
we meditated with monks
in Ladakh, stretched with the yogis
in Delhi, and together moved far away
from our roots.

And now he's returned.
T'shuvah.
From sin to repentance.
His prayer shawl, packed away
since the day of our wedding
fifteen years ago,
hangs prominently now among his suits.
The *gi* he wore to aikido
abandoned on a top shelf.

I look at this man
and again I ask,
who is he?
who has he become?
And what
wrapped comfortably
in my smug modernity
scares me?

My husband's transformation struck me as odd. I did not understand his reciting Hebrew prayers at all hours of the day and night, his wrapping *tefillin*, the black leather straps around his head, his left arm and one of his fingers. I knew that halfway measures never suited him, that when he did something, it was always with a full heart. But adopting orthodox Judaism felt alien to me.

My husband's return to religion may have been one of the fissures in our twenty-two-year marriage. I can't say for sure. It takes another five years or so for the marriage to end, and this, too, comes as a surprise. The signs are all there, but I choose not to read them. I suspect that I am better at busying myself with work and with parenting, better at teaching classes and writing books than examining the underside of relationships. Perhaps, like my mother and sister, I am actually more concerned with appearances than with what lies underneath. Whatever the reasons, or the blind spots, I do not see what is coming. I capture the changes, though, in a poem I write after we separate.

After 25 Years of Marriage, Arthur Becomes Artie

The day you changed your name
From Arthur to Artie
I should have known.

I should have seen it coming—
Not only a new name
But also a new hairstyle,
The curls I loved cut off,
Your thick black hair flat now,

Slicked back against your skull,
Like the coat of some cat
Left out in the rain.

You morphed
From clinical psychologist
To multi-level marketer,
Selling vitamins
And skin care products
On the internet—
How blind could I be?

The cover story was a good one:
You wanted to make money
So you could return to Viet Nam
So you could build schools
And churches
In a personal act of retribution,
Repairing the damage
You thought you had done.

But, really,
You were reinventing yourself,
A delayed midlife crisis.
It should not have surprised me
That in all this reinvention:
A new name
A new look
A new professional identity
Complete with a gold business card
You'd also want
A new woman.

My husband left, one day, to live with another woman. Ah, that had
certainly been a secret. It would have been easy to see myself as the
victim, the unsuspecting wife. But while I did not suspect, I also knew
it takes two people to make a marriage succeed—or fail. Over the
years, we grew apart. We stopped confiding in each other; we stopped

finding each other as fascinating as we once had. I don't think I would have ever initiated the break, even in those moments when I recognized my own unhappiness. But having the break thrust upon me freed me in ways I could not have imagined. As we were separating, my husband predicted that one day, I'd be grateful to him for making this move. In truth, I am.

It takes a while for me to regroup, to find the path I now want to pursue. I talk endlessly to family and friends, clean my house from top to bottom, travel by myself and with others, and begin to study the flute. One summer, on advice from my brother, I take a trip to British Columbia. There, I chance upon a piece of property that is for sale. I realize that I can afford it, and while it is far from my home in New York, I know there is something right about staking a claim to something I want. Had I always wanted a house on an island? Is this another secret buried deep within? What gives me the confidence to take this step? In another poem, written while I am leading a writing workshop in 2004, along the Pacific coast in Big Sur, California, I try to understand what this step means to me.

Where Contraction Dies

I have known the pain of contraction:
The squeezing into small places,
The desire to please,
To accommodate,
To make myself over
So that I'll fit
Into this man's world.

I have known this pain
Since I was three, five, ten.
Each year, it became easier to read the signs,
To obey the commands:
"Be good."
"Be nice."
"Do well."
"Smile."
"Save."

I got good at it:
At pretending,
At looking the other way,
At denying what was true for me.
So good,
I almost lost my soul.

Until one day,
Almost by chance,
I said yes to a place,
To a house
On an island
In British Columbia.

I've spent only three days there,
Slept in the bed
On the second floor
For only three nights,
Sat on the wooden stairs
That lead to the beach below
For only one
Star-lit evening.

And yet
When I entered the house
For the first time
I cried.

This house
Came to me
The way good things often come
By surprise.

It stands high on a bluff,
Overlooking a bay.
The snow-capped mountains
Of Vancouver Island

Visible in the distance.
It is enclosed by a carved wooden fence
Built to keep out the deer,
Graceful creatures who eat the flowers
Whose names
I don't yet know.

On the land are apple trees,
Three different kinds,
An outdoor shower,
136 steps that wind down
To the rocky beach below.

It speaks to me,
This house,
Of peace,
Of serenity,
Of expansion.
Here, it says,
Your soul can soar
Like the eagles
Who glide on air currents,
And then settle themselves,
Stoically,
Eyes unblinking,
In the treetops.

This is where,
It says,
Contraction dies.

Looking back, through these poems, I see a young girl struggling to find her way, someone who was brought up to please her parents, particularly the men in her life, someone who wasn't particularly comfortable taking risks, who preferred to fit in and to play it safe unless her values were threatened. And then, if pushed hard enough, she stood up and said no.

This girl grew up, got married, had children, taught writing, traveled, and became an adult. She kept herself busy with projects, with work, with family. It was—and still is—a good life. What mattered to her—and still does—is that life has meaning, that actions have purpose, that she continues to grow and to explore both the sharp—and the soft—edges of her life.

Now, as I compose the final section to this chapter, I do so from the house in British Columbia described above. I do it not alone but with a partner at my side, a man who shares this journey of discovery with me. This relationship, almost five years old now, also comes as a surprise, and with it the revelation that love knows no age limit. Now when I write poems, I explore, more often than not, moments of pleasure and intimacy. I won't include them here, not because they are embarrassing or painful, but because they are private, as some writing must be.